Better Behavior

for Ages 2–10

Small Miracles
That Work Like Magic

Tara Egan, EdD

www.lessonladder.com

21 Orient Street, Melrose, MA 02176

Published 2013
Printed in the United States
1 2 3 4 5 6 7 13 12 11 10 09 08

Lesson Ladder: an imprint of XAMonline, Inc.
21 Orient Street, Melrose, MA 02176

Toll Free: 1-800-301-4647
Fax: 1-617-583-5552
Email: customerservice@lessonladder.com
Web: www.lessonladder.com

Text: **Tara Egan, EdD**

Illustrations: Angela Montoya, Moira Gillis Gray, Nathan Saylor, Rachel Enos, and Terrie Cundiff
Front cover: ThinkStock/78401290
Back cover: ThinkStock/152311836
Book design: iiCREATIVE
Production: nSight, Inc.
Project management: Elizabeth St. Germain
Acquisitions editor: Beth Kaufman

Library of Congress Catalog Card Number:
(pending)
Tara Egan, EdD
Better Behavior for Ages 2-10: Small Miracles That Work Like Magic   188 pp., ill.

1. Title

2. Parenting

3. Child psychology

4. Behavior modification

5. Child rearing

HQ755.8 E43 2013   649.64 E282 2013
ISBN: 978-098486-5772

Dedication

To Savannah and Declan
Thank you for letting me write about parenting you. I'm so proud to be your mom.
I love you both so much.

To Mer
You make me stronger.

To Mom and Dad
I think you were the first people to refer to me as a "writer."
Thank you for your encouragement and support, especially throughout the past two years.

To Jon
You came into my life at exactly the right time.

To the Staff at Lesson Ladder
An especially big "thank you" to my project manager, Beth Kaufman, whose passion for
the parent was paramount. She and her team have helped me produce a quality book.

To iiCreative
You designed such a visually appealing product.

About the Author

Tara Egan, EdD, founder of *Charlotte Parent Coaching*, has over twelve years of experience as a school psychologist and parent coach. In addition to her work with individual families, she has taught at the college level and worked extensively with public schools, private schools, and mental health facilities. Dr. Egan has worked in several states, including Maryland, Minnesota, New York, and North Carolina. In addition, she has provided training to individuals and groups on topics such as best practices in parenting, behavioral management of children, navigating the special education process in the schools, and academic and behavioral interventions for use in the classroom setting.

Dr. Egan has two children, a girl and a boy, and enjoys reading, writing, and exercise. Every day her children remind her that of all her job responsibilities, being a parent is her most important role.

Contents

PREFACE ix

Chapter 1: When I Have Children, They Will Never...

Asking for Parenting Help 5
Defining Misbehavior. 7
Describing Misbehavior. 7
Distribution of Misbehavior 8
Goals of This Book. 10
How to Read This Book 10
  Part I: Behavior: What Every Parent Needs to Know (Chapters 1–3). 11
  Part II: Key Concepts Related to the Behavioral Model (Chapters 4–7). 11
  Part III: Applying What You've Learned (Chapters 8 and 9). 11
Audience 11
Let's Talk About "We" and "Us" 12
The "Bad" Word. 13
Themes 13
  Theme 1: The Best Way to Deal with Misbehavior Is to Prevent It. 13
  Theme 2: Don't Let Your Children Do Today What You Don't Want Them to Do Tomorrow. . . .14
  Theme 3: Good Behavior Has to Be Taught. Good Behavior Has to Be Role-Modeled. Good
  Behavior Has to Be Reinforced. Often.. 16
Key Points Discussed in Chapter 1 16

Chapter 2: Understanding Why Children Misbehave

Why Children Misbehave. 19
  Children Don't Know How to Demonstrate the "Right" Skill 19
  The "Right" Activity is Too Hard or Unpleasant and Is Perceived as Punishment 20
  The "Right" Behavior Is Ignored. 20
  The Misbehavior Gets Them Attention 20
  There Are No Consequences for Misbehavior. 21
Variables That Contribute to a Child's Misbehavior. 21
  Child Variables 22
  Parental Expectations 22
  Societal Expectations 23
  Environmental Variables 23
Positive Reinforcement, Negative Reinforcement, and Punishment 23
"Internal Needs" Met by Misbehavior 25
  Six Categories of "Needs". 25
Examining the Whole Child 28
  The Whole Child 28
  Sleep 29
  Nutrition 32
  Sensory Issues 35
Final Thoughts. 39
Key Points Discussed in Chapter 2 39

Chapter 3: Empowering Parents

Transitions and Advance Warning 42
    Types of Transitions. 42
    Tips for Giving Advance Warning and Setting Clear Expectations .43
Attention 45
Be Prepared. 46
    Tips for Being Prepared. 46
Realistic Behavioral Expectations 47
    Factors to Consider When Setting Realistic Behavioral Expectations 47
Mood/Attitude 51
Take Responsibility 52
Key Points Discussed in Chapter 3 53

Chapter 4: Reinforcing Positive Behavior

Basic Types of Reinforcement. 56
    Physical 56
    Verbal. 57
    Privileges 57
    Time 58
    Tangible Rewards 58
How to Choose the Type of Reinforcement 59
Tips for Using Reinforcement Effectively. 62
    Use Secondary Praise. Children Love It, and It Works 64
Intrinsic vs. Extrinsic Motivation 64
Final Thoughts. 66
Key Points Discussed in Chapter 4 66

Chapter 5: Adopting a Nurturing Communication Style and Encouraging Better Listening

Parenting Styles 69
    Authoritarian. 70
    Permissive 70
    Uninvolved 71
    Authoritative 72
Nurturing Communication. 73
    What Is It? 73
    Components of Nurturing Language 73
    Adopting a Nurturing Communication Style 74
Encouraging Better Listening 78
Tips to Improve Your Child's Listening. 78
Final Thoughts. 85
Key Points Discussed in Chapter 5 85

Chapter 6: Utilizing Natural vs. Logical Consequences and Coping with Power Struggles

Natural Consequences 90
   Determining Natural Consequences 91
Logical Consequences 92
Intrinsic and Extrinsic Motivation Revisited. 93
Coping with Power Struggles 94
Top Ten Tips to Avoid Power Struggles 97
   How and When to Factor in Your Child's Opinion 100
Final Thoughts. 108
Key Points Discussed in Chapter 6 109

Chapter 7: Understanding and Navigating Temper Outbursts

What Is a Temper Outburst? 112
   How Temper Outbursts Evolve with Age 113
Why Children Have Temper Outbursts. 113
The Seven Stages of a Temper Outburst for a Child 115
The Role of Parents During Temper Outbursts 116
   The Seven Stages of a Temper Outburst for a Parent. 116
The Trigger 117
   Slow Triggers 117
   Fast Triggers. 118
   The Parent's Role in Recognizing Triggers 119
The Last Chance to Prevent It Part 119
   The Parent's Role: Simple Strategies to Avoid a Temper Outburst. 120
The Ugly Part. 123
   The Parent's Role During the Ugly Part 123
   Soothing Techniques for Parents during the Ugly Part 124
The Turning Point. 126
   The Parent's Role During the Turning Point 126
The Soothing/Self-Soothing Part. 126
   The Parent's Role in Helping Soothe Their Child. 127
The Learning Opportunity/Teaching Moment 128
   The Parent's Role in the Teaching Moment 128
The Kiss and Make Up Part 129
   The Parent's Role in the Making Up Part 130
Question: What about the Children Who Can "Turn Off" an Outburst Extremely Quickly? . .130
Don't Be Frightened of Temper Outbursts. 131
Key Points Discussed in Chapter 7 132

Chapter 8: How to Use Punishment Effectively

Five Necessary Components for Effective Punishment 136

Pitfalls to Punishment 138

Time-out 139
   What Is Time-out? 139
   The Four Myths of Time-out 140
   Seven Steps for an Effective Time-out. 142
   Time-out in a Public Place. 147
   A "Self" Time-out 148

Apologizing: Should We Force Our Child to Apologize? 148
   Pros of "Making" Your Child Apologize 149
   Cons of "Making" Your Child Apologize 149

Key Points Discussed in Chapter 8 151

Chapter 9: The Parent Toolbox: Applying What We Know

Transitions 153

Bedtime. 156
   Preparing for a New Bedtime Routine 156
   Transitioning to the New Bedtime Routine 158
   Troubleshooting. 159

Taking Care of Personal Belongings/Cleaning Up 161

Dealing with Whining. 163

Restaurant Etiquette 164

How to Say "Yes" as a Way to Motivate Your Child. 167

Fostering Respect 168

Common Behavioral Strategies to Avoid 169
   Token Economy 169
   Competition 171

Conclusion. 172

Key Points Discussed in Chapter 9 173

REFERENCES 175

PREFACE

The inspiration for *Better Behavior: Small Miracles That Work Like Magic* has been simmering throughout the length of my career—starting with my training as a teacher, progressing through my decade of work as a school psychologist, and expanding as I settled into my role as a parent coach.

In 2011, I established a parent coaching practice (www.charlotteparentcoaching .com) dedicated to supporting parents and families through a myriad of issues including behavioral challenges, social skill deficits, and specialized learning needs. This new venture gave me the opportunity to work closely with individual families and conduct a series of parenting seminars. The seminars that typically garnered the largest audiences were those that addressed the behavioral needs of preschool- and elementary school-aged children. Discussions tended to focus on issues such as coping with power struggles and temper outbursts, improving overall communication between parent and child, and effectively administering reinforcement and consequences.

As my influence in the community expanded and more parents saw the immediate benefit of implementing the strategies I suggested, parents and colleagues began urging me to write a book. Initially I demurred, indicating that the primary goal of my work was to provide *individualized* recommendations to families. I wasn't interested in touting a "cookie-cutter" approach to addressing behavioral issues. I observed each child personally, interviewed each parent and teacher, and considered each family's strengths and weaknesses. As a result, I designed interventions that were specific to that particular child and family. That, I felt, was the reason why my clients demonstrated such exceptional growth.

As I gained more experience as a parent coach, however, I realized something important. While I did, in fact, personalize each recommendation, there were also overriding principles that I espoused—most of which originated from what I refer to as a "nurturing communication style" throughout this book. With the help of my brilliant team of editors at Lesson Ladder, Inc. (consisting of Beth Kaufman, Corbin Lewars, and Kristen Mellitt, specifically), I was able to tease out the underlying foundations of my behavioral model while protecting the decision-making process that evolves when I work with an individual family. This book, my editors pointed out, could be used as a way to reach more families.

Together, we spent the next several months crafting a behavioral model that can be used by all families. I'm very proud of our work. It's meaningful, different than other resources currently available, and remains true to the vision I have for all my clients. All families, I feel, have the ability to be healthy and happy—some just need a little support and guidance through the challenging times.

Tara Egan, EdD

Look for this bonus section in every chapter!

True Tale

True stories from Dr. Tara's life and work that illustrate key text themes.

True Tale

I learned about my son's sensory issues, particularly with regard to noise and feeling crowded, when he was about 18 months old. He screamed relentlessly when I brought him to a busy food court at the mall. Finally, I left to walk him to the car. Upon exiting the mall, his tears stopped immediately. From that point on, I have always been mindful about asking him to participate in activities that are excessively noisy.

Better Behavior

for Ages 2–10

Chapter 1

When I Have Children, They Will Never...

Prior to having children, I was a different psychologist. Although I considered myself to be well-trained, empathic, and a good communicator, I didn't have the perspective of a parent. To be honest, I was afflicted with a mild case of "When I Have Children, They Will Never" Syndrome. I thought you simply needed to tell children how to behave, and they would.

But upon the birth of my first child, a little girl, I quickly learned that simply telling a child how to behave isn't enough. After all, some children are extremely strong-willed. Some need to be shown over and over and over. Some need to directly experience the consequences of their behavior before they learn how to modify it. Some develop differently and need to be taught in a specialized way.

Regardless, with the birth of my child came the realization that one should *never* utter the words, "When I have children, they will never..." Out loud, that is. Think them if you want. Write them down and seal them in a time capsule if you must. Spray paint them on an anonymous wall in the inner city. Carve them into a tree. Etch them on a bathroom wall with your pocket knife.

But you should never say them aloud.

These words will haunt you throughout the night after your child has a temper outburst in the middle of your sister's wedding ceremony. They will cause your face to flush with shame when your mother-in-law reminds you of these words after your children act like violent offenders in a restaurant in front of your husband's entire extended family. They will ring in your ears when your child's teacher calls to inform you that your second grader called her peer a "b*tch" on the playground. They will prevent you from reaching for the phone to seek comfort from your mother after learning that your son regaled his friend's family with stories about all the times he's vomited after eating something you prepared.

Prior to becoming a parent, our kids are perfect—primarily due to our perfect parenting.

But then we actually become parents, and we realize how very mistaken we were. We learn that there is certainly no child who is perfect, and there is certainly no parent who is perfect, either. Even the most attentive, brightest, most experienced parents sometimes make parenting decisions that they regret immediately. There are times when we feel helpless as parents, especially if we see that our child is not growing into the child we expected him or her to be.

If you're reading this book, chances are you may be experiencing extreme frustration with your child's behavior. You may feel as though you're failing them. You may be tired of hearing family, friends, and strangers comment on or give advice about the misbehavior of your young child. You may be struggling to enjoy your time with your child because so many of your interactions are fraught with turmoil. You may feel that others—and maybe even you—find it hard to see the likeability of your child.

When parents initially contact me, common phrases I hear are:

> *"I'm scared I'm doing this [parenting] wrong."*
> *"It's hard to like my daughter sometimes."*
> *"Other kids always seem better behaved than mine."*
> *"My spouse doesn't think there is a problem, but I do."*
> *"If he's like this now, what is he going to be like in five years?"*

When I was in graduate school, I once attended a meeting where a group of school professionals were discussing the misbehavior of a student named Marcus. He was a kindergartener who was exhibiting extreme behavioral outbursts in the classroom, characterized by yelling, crying, and throwing objects.

During the meeting, the conversation focused on how the student was negatively impacting his peers, his teachers, the administrators, and the school property. At one point, my supervisor asked my opinion about the situation at hand. I replied, "It's probably really hard to be one of Marcus's classmates right now. After all, it's hard to concentrate in a classroom while another student is always having outbursts." Everyone agreed readily. I continued, "It's probably also really hard to be one of his teachers, as it's hard to instruct an entire classroom of children when one student is demanding so much attention." Once again, the adults in the room nodded somberly. Finally, I said, "But I suspect that it's hardest of all to be Marcus. After all, he's the one who has completely lost control of his emotions. He probably spends most of his day feeling angry, frightened, and alone."

> We live in a society in which parenthood is often treated as a competition.

Misbehavior exhibited by children is hard on everyone. Because dealing with a defiant child is so frustrating, I think adults sometimes forget that *being* the defiant child is also extremely difficult.

Parenting is one role in which our self-perception is based on the behavior and well-being of another—our child. In other areas of our lives, such as being an employee, our evaluation of ourselves is based on our behavior and our achievements, all of which are somewhat in our control. When our child suffers, we suffer. We suffer because it hurts us to see our children hurting, and we hurt because we're disappointed in ourselves for not having the foresight to protect our child. I invite you to base your self-worth as a parent on your responsiveness to your child when he or she is struggling, rather than berate yourself over the struggle.

Asking for Parenting Help

In our society, it's acceptable to support our child's abilities through the use of a soccer coach, a gymnastics instructor, or a math tutor. We can take our child to the doctor for allergies, an orthodontist for braces, or an optometrist for glasses.

The pressure that we put on ourselves to be "good" parents is enormous. And with single parenthood on the rise, both parents often working outside the home, media use prevalent among even very young children, and school violence receiving increased public attention, many parents face extraordinary challenges.

> It's the "good" parents who ask for help when their family is struggling.

Terms like "helicopter parenting," "permissive parenting," and "attachment parenting" are commonplace, and debates surrounding organic nutrition, vaccination use, educational policies, and nontraditional family structures are rampant and divisive.

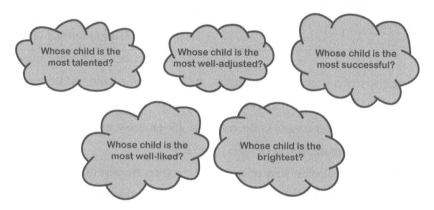

But sometimes the best way to support our child is to obtain support for *ourselves*—the parents. Prior to parenthood, we have no idea that parenthood will be fraught with so many difficult decisions and obstacles. We have no idea that we *need* to prepare, let alone *how* to.

Then baby comes home. A tiny, squeaking baby, whose needs seem so simple—eat, sleep, and poop. We're led to believe that caring for a child is somehow innate or instinctual. Parents are just supposed to *know* how to meet their child's needs. I mean, how hard is it to get your 14-month-old to eat, am I right? (Ahem.)

The last I checked, responding calmly to a toddler smacking you in the face with his shoe after you tell him to stop screaming in the car is not instinctual. Keeping your temper after your 10-year-old answers your polite request with a disdainful "Forget it, Mom," is not innate. Knowing what to do when you learn that your child has been bullying other children at school is not automatic. Parenting in these situations takes effort and mindfulness that comes naturally to only the smallest portion of parents.

Understandably, asking for help with parenting can be associated with guilt, shame, and a sense of failure. And oftentimes when I'm interacting with my own children, I stop to ask myself, "What advice would I give to another parent in this situation?" Once I ask myself this question, my emotional mind usually responds, "But I don't want to!" Making a decision designed to change my child's behavior takes a commitment of time, effort, and patience that I may not feel prepared to make at that exact moment.

As a parent, your sense of responsibility to help your child is fierce and all-consuming. You not only worry about their functioning today—this moment—but you also worry about their future, their overall potential for success, and their happiness.

Defining Misbehavior

Throughout this book, the term "misbehavior" will be used. Misbehavior refers to all problem behavior, undesirable behavior, or behavior that you want to stop, reduce, or change in some way.

Misbehavior is usually behavior that causes parents to feel annoyed, frustrated, angry, or worried. Parents often use the following words and phrases to describe misbehavior: temper tantrums, talking back, whining, defiance, failing to complete chores or homework, misusing toys or other belongings, not following directions, poor listening, physical aggression, or poor social skills.

Although there are infinite ways in which children can misbehave, most parents agree that misbehavior is behavior that impairs their child's functioning and/or the functioning of their family.

Describing Misbehavior

A review of current research indicates that it's difficult to determine the exact nature and frequency of misbehavior in the home setting. After all, researchers would need to rely on parents to identify the misbehavior, describe it, and collect data on its frequency. To some extent, misbehavior is subjective, as it may be defined differently by each family. Oftentimes, the behavior that's perceived by adults to be the most troublesome is that which can be classified as annoying or resulting from failing to listen to directives. Regardless, it is nearly impossible to assess behavior objectively, as it often elicits very strong emotions from the parent.

I grew up in a home with a mother, a father, and three brothers. In our home, mild aggression in the form of wrestling, horseplay, and physical games was accepted—even encouraged. In my neighbor's home, consisting of a single mother with two little girls, physical aggression was nearly unheard of; it would have been shocking if one of the little girls had playfully jumped on her sleeping sister or if they had arm-wrestled each other for the last piece of pie.

As this True Tale illustrates, what is acceptable in one home may be considered misbehavior in another. In the school setting, however, all children are asked to follow the same set of rules and expectations. Therefore, misbehavior is more easily observed and categorized by teachers and other school professionals. In a study conducted by Sugai and Horner (1999), it was determined that 5 percent of the students account for 40.4 percent of discipline referrals. This statistic suggests that only a small portion of students demonstrate misbehavior that is severe and/or chronic enough to warrant a discipline referral and/or attention from an administrator.

In fact, research indicates that in the school setting:

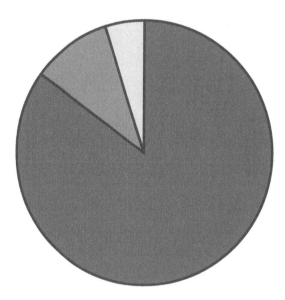

- 80 to 90 percent of children will respond to general classroom management.

- 5 to 15 percent of children will respond successfully to informal behavioral planning on a group or individual level.

- Fewer than 5 percent of children require the use of specialized behavioral planning to address severe and chronic misbehavior.

Responding to Misbehavior in a School Setting

Distribution of Misbehavior

As the diagram above indicates, there are degrees of misbehavior ranging from very mild to severe. While all children misbehave from time to time, the percentage of those who misbehave to a significant extent is minimal. The remainder of the time, the vast majority of misbehavior can be addressed with the consistent application of high-quality behavioral management techniques.

1. **Eighty to 90 percent of children will respond successfully to general classroom management.**

   This statistic indicates that although all children misbehave on occasion, the vast majority of misbehavior can be prevented or addressed through the use of best practices in classroom management, such as creating appropriate classroom rules, managing time efficiently, keeping students engaged, and handling disruptions effectively.

   How this pertains to parents: All children misbehave on occasion. However, most children will respond favorably when parents establish clear, age-appropriate expectations; manipulate the environmental variables so that children are positioned to experience success; maintain consistent consequences for misbehavior; and use praise and reinforcement appropriately.

2. **Five to 15 percent of children will respond successfully to informal behavioral planning on a group or individual level.**

   This statistic refers to the child who is more strong-willed or moderately resistant to the general behavioral principles established by an effective teacher in the school setting. This child may need:

   - More attention/encouragement from the teacher
   - More practice to learn the appropriate behavioral response
   - Less reinforcement of misbehavior and/or increased reinforcement of positive behavior

   How this pertains to parents: At home, this child may require more instruction with regard to positive behavior and increased structure to help him or her adhere to behavioral expectations. In addition, this child may experience more severe temper outbursts or logical/natural consequences before understanding and accepting the boundaries established by their parents.

3. **Fewer than 5 percent of children require the use of specialized behavioral planning to address severe and chronic misbehavior.**

   This statistic refers to the children who exhibit significant misbehavior in the school setting. These children may cause significant disruption to the education of their peers. In addition, the time, attention, and resources of the school administration may be taxed due to the behavioral demands of these children. These children will require specialized behavioral programming to address their misbehavior.

   How this pertains to parents: The misbehavior of these children will certainly warrant outside behavioral support, as it will severely impact the overall functioning of the family.

Goals of This Book

This book is written to serve as a guide to parents who are struggling to manage their child's behavior. The goals of this book are three-fold:

1. To provide parents with *preventative* and *proactive* strategies so that misbehavior can be handled before it occurs or before it becomes a pattern

2. To provide parents with *reactive* strategies designed to address problem behavior that is already occurring and needs to be discontinued

3. To provide parents with a specific behavioral model that can be used in the home to ensure that good behavior is the rule, not an exception

How to Read This Book

My goal is to provide you with a resource that's understandable, practical, and relevant to your children and parenting style. I hope to convey concepts that are easy to recall and implement, and to present a behavioral approach that is cohesive and applicable to all kinds of families and homes.

This book is divided into three sections:

Part I: Behavior: What Every Parent Needs to Know (Chapters 1–3)

These chapters introduce the book and provide a preview of the overall rationale behind the behavioral model. Chapter 1 will define and describe misbehavior, place it in a larger framework as far as frequency and severity, and discuss three overall themes that will be revisited throughout this book. Chapter 2 will discuss why children misbehave, define the concepts of reinforcement and punishment, and illustrate how behavior relates to an "internal need" within the child. Chapter 3 will focus on empowering parents, helping them recognize that there are numerous ways in which a parent can adjust the environment in order to "set the stage" for a child's behavioral success.

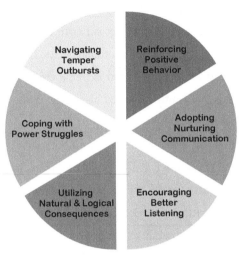

Dr. Tara Egan's Behavioral Model

Part II: Key Concepts Related to the Behavioral Model (Chapters 4–7)

These chapters are the heart of the behavioral model. They describe the six principles of the behavioral model, designed to create a comprehensive approach to address the most common misbehaviors.

Part III: Applying What You've Learned (Chapters 8 and 9)

The final two chapters are designed to illustrate how to apply the concepts discussed during Part II. Specifically, Chapter 8 will discuss how to use punishment effectively and Chapter 9 will provide recommendations about very specific behavioral scenarios.

Audience

Although the principles described in this book can be applied to children of all ages, this book is most likely to resonate with parents of children between the ages of 24 months and 10 years. The examples provided and the anecdotes shared are most relevant for toddlers, preschoolers, and elementary-school-aged children, rather than adolescents or young adults.

It's also important to note that the examples provided in this book are based on real-life experiences with children who are typically developing. More specifically, this book is written for the parent whose child does not suffer from *significant* cognitive or emotional delays. If your child has a moderate or severe form of autism, has experienced extreme emotional trauma, or has a medical diagnosis that has significantly impacted his or her development, then this book may not be as helpful to you.

> The anecdotes shared in this book are based on real-life examples: real children, real parents, real misbehavior, and real solutions.

However, I also want to note that "normal" or "average" are not terms embraced in this book. The term "typically developing" may be used, as I feel this term refers to a broad range of behavior and encompasses the vast majority of children, even those who demonstrate characteristics consistent with attention Attention Deficit/Hyperactivity Disorder (ADHD), Asperger's Syndrome, learning disabilities, mild to moderate emotional problems, or mild to moderate social skill weaknesses.

Let's Talk About "We" and "Us"

You'll find that throughout this book, I often refer to parents as "we" and "us." This is because author and psychologist aside, I am a parent first. Although there is no role of which I'm more proud, I'll freely admit that it is *hard*.

> It is the truly exceptional parents who ask for help. I have never once worked with a "bad" parent.

Parents are expected to make dozens of decisions each day pertaining to their child (or children)—decisions that, conceivably, shape who their children become as people. The responsibility can feel enormous, especially when we realize that it's virtually impossible to make the right decisions all the time.

When new acquaintances learn of my work as a parent coach, I'm often asked, "Are the parents with whom you work really incompetent? I mean, it's the 'bad' parents who need you, right?" My response is always the same: "It is the truly exceptional parents who ask for help. I have never once worked with a 'bad' parent."

I've found that the parents who seek help are wholeheartedly invested in their family's mental health and ability to function well. These parents are typically extremely motivated and receptive to my recommendations. They've approached me in order to learn strategies so that the entire family dynamic will improve, and they respond to my suggestions with enthusiasm and patience. In short, they are excellent parents.

The "Bad" Word

"Tell Daddy how bad you were at school today."

"Her daughters are adorable, but her son is bad."

"I'm sorry I was so bad today, Mom."

The word "bad" is a strong word to use when describing a child. It implies that the child's character is innately flawed—that the child is somehow less than, inferior, or substandard. It suggests that his or her behavior is hardwired—unable to be managed or improved upon.

In contrast, all children, even those who demonstrate extreme misbehavior, can make behavioral improvements. All children can benefit from mindful parenting.

Therefore, the word "bad," because of the stigma it holds, is not a word that will be used in this book.

A child may make poor choices.

A child may have been naughty.

A child may misbehave.

A child may exhibit problem behavior.

But a child is not "bad."

Themes

Throughout this book, there are several themes or overall messages that will be discussed.

Theme 1: The Best Way to Deal with Misbehavior Is to Prevent It.

As new parents with friends who also have young children, we often have the opportunity to hear about the common misadventures of children. Everyone has a story about a time when a parent forgot some crucial safety rule that could have been catastrophic. Or a tale about a temper outburst at an inopportune time. Or an anecdote about how we inadvertently reinforced a behavior that was undesirable.

Some misbehavior is preventable simply because it's easy to anticipate. For example:

- Forgetting to bring a favorite stuffed animal on vacation is likely to result in tears or a temper outburst.
- Leaving markers or scissors unattended is likely to lead to their misuse.
- Sitting in a waiting room for one hour at lunch time is likely to result in whining and/or tears.

The fact is some misbehavior can be predicted. As parents, we can anticipate when misbehavior is likely to occur based on our child's personality, their developmental age, and their past misbehavior. For example, we know that children between the ages of one and four are likely to engage in a temper outburst if asked to stop a fun activity. We know a child who forfeited a nap is likely to be unpleasant all afternoon.

Oftentimes, we can prevent misbehavior through the use of mindful parenting—changing how we interact with our environment or our child so we can position him or her to achieve success. We will discuss this topic extensively in Chapter 3.

Theme 2: Don't Let Your Children Do Today What You Don't Want Them to Do Tomorrow.

Sometimes, we permit our small children to engage in behavior that we'd never allow our older children to do. For example, a toddler jumping on the sofa while you stand by safely monitoring him seems harmless, right? But fast-forward to when your 100-pound 12-year-old jumping just as enthusiastically on the sofa may cause significant damage to the sofa.

> Just because your child is "too little to understand" does not mean s/he should be permitted to misbehave. This just means that you have more time to teach him/her.

Now, tell me: Which is the day that jumping on the couch transfers from being "acceptable" behavior to "unacceptable" behavior? When he reaches the age of six? When his weight tops 60 pounds? When you can hear the thump of his jumping through the ceiling when you're doing laundry in the basement?

Also consider: Will he be confused as to why the rules have changed? Is he likely to be compliant? Is he more likely to demonstrate carelessness with other furniture after he's been permitted to jump on the couch?

This is a simple example, of course, but it illustrates the concept that if you do not want your child to engage in a specific behavior at a later time, do not permit him to do it today. Even if he's too little to understand why he shouldn't behave that way, he's more likely to be compliant if he's been exposed to a consistent behavioral expectation. Eventually, he will be old enough to understand your rationale.

True Tale

When my daughter was very small (about 18 months old), I lived in a three-story townhome with a garage. I had to carry my child and any other belongings (such as groceries) up a large flight of stairs to reach the main level. Typically, I'd get my daughter out of the car, set her just inside the door to the house, and go back to get my belongings. If I had an arm free to carry her, I would. If my hands were full, I'd encourage her to climb the stairs with me following closely behind.

One day, I lifted her up and let her press the button on the wall to shut the garage door. Within days, she lost all interest in willingly toddling into the house and up the stairs, demanding that I drop everything, lift her up to press the button, and then set her down and wait while she watched the door slowly creep closed. It was infuriating, as the relatively simple task of getting into the house was now lengthy and more physically demanding.

I should never have done it the first time, as it's not surprising that a small child would find that appealing. Because she wasn't old enough to understand that it was a one-time behavior that was not conducive to daily life, temper outbursts erupted if I wasn't immediately accommodating. I eventually "solved" the problem by refusing to pick her up and let her press the button and sticking with this resolution. Within a few days—and several temper outbursts later—she stopped expecting to be able to do it.

From that incident, I learned to be very mindful of what I permitted my daughter to do. If it wasn't a behavior that I felt could or should be maintained, then I didn't permit it in the first place.

Theme 3: Good Behavior Has to Be Taught. Good Behavior Has to Be Role-Modeled. Good Behavior Has to Be Reinforced. Often.

This third theme will be visited repeatedly throughout this book.

We'll talk about how children need to know *how* to behave before they can be *expected* to behave.

We'll talk about how good behavior cannot be simply *discussed*; it needs to be *demonstrated* over and over, preferably by you and by other important individuals in children's lives.

We'll talk about how children need to be *motivated* to display good behavior. More specifically, we'll talk about the various ways in which behavior can be encouraged and the frequency that's necessary to foster positive behavior.

Misbehavior can be willful. It can be destructive. It can be unhealthy. It can be frustrating or anger-provoking. But misbehavior can be improved.

We have a lot to talk about.

So let's get started.

Key Points Discussed in Chapter 1

- Sometimes the best way to support a child is for the parents to ask for help. No one is a perfect parent.

- Misbehavior refers to all problem behavior, undesirable behavior, or behavior that you want to stop, reduce, or change in some way. Misbehavior is usually behavior that causes parents to feel annoyed, frustrated, angry, or worried.

- Misbehavior is subjective, as it may be defined differently by each family. However, 80 to 90 percent of children are likely to respond favorably to good, solid, preventative discipline strategies.

- This book will describe a specific behavioral model that can be applied to any child and any home. It can be used to prevent misbehavior, as well as to address current misbehavior.

- There are several themes that we will focus on throughout this book:
  1. The best way to deal with misbehavior is to prevent it.
  2. Don't let your children do today what you don't want them to do tomorrow.
  3. Good behavior has to be taught. Good behavior has to be role-modeled. Good behavior has to be reinforced. Often.

Notes:

Chapter 2

Understanding Why Children Misbehave

Why Children Misbehave

Children misbehave for numerous reasons.

Children Don't Know How to Demonstrate the "Right" Skill

Children need to know how to engage in a certain behavior before they will do it independently. All too often, parents will say, "Don't do that!" but will not give direct instruction on what *to* do. For example, parents will say, "Stop acting naughty in the restaurant!" but will not

> There is motivation behind nearly all misbehavior. Preventing future misbehavior is dependent upon understanding this motivation.

describe or teach the behavior that is expected (remain in your seat, use your utensils, and speak with an inside voice).

The "Right" Activity is Too Hard or Unpleasant and Is Perceived as Punishment

True Tale

When my daughter was about two years old, I directed her to eat her green beans. She informed me that they were "gross" and refused to eat them. After being told that she would not be permitted to leave the table without eating two bites, she attempted to eat them. After chewing on them gingerly for a few seconds, she vomited and burst into tears. It was months before I could convince her to try green beans again, as she equated eating green beans with feeling sick. In this example, she perceived the "right" behavior to be too unpleasant. Although this doesn't suggest that we should never insist that our children eat their vegetables, we should be mindful of our children's perceptions of the acceptable behavior.

Another example of this might be when a child delays or refuses to do his homework. Upon closer investigation, you learn that he struggles to understand the directions, can't maintain his attention for more than a few minutes, and gets fatigued easily when asked to do the same task over and over (like a series of math problems). Despite the fact that he understands that he's expected to do his homework, he perceives it to be too hard and reacts by avoiding it.

The "Right" Behavior Is Ignored

When children are behaving appropriately, we often take it for granted and don't make a point to praise or reinforce the positive behavior. We may think, "Why do I need to praise them when they are doing exactly what they are supposed to be doing? No one praises me for getting ready for work on time or taking my dishes to the sink." However, because children are still in the process of figuring out which behavior should and will become part of their regular repertoire of behavior, it's very important to send a clear message to the child that says, "Keep doing this."

The Misbehavior Gets Them Attention

While we tend to ignore the "right" behavior, we oftentimes give excessive attention to the misbehavior. When our child is behaving appropriately, we may actually pay less attention to him or her because we take it for granted or because the good behavior permits us to be less vigilant. In contrast, when he or she misbehaves, we may be extremely vigilant in the form of offering corrective feedback, distraction, or appeasement. Most children would

> **Attention is inherently reinforcing. Most children would rather have negative attention (such as being scolded) than no attention at all.**

rather have negative attention than no attention at all. If we're attending to the misbehavior, we're actually reinforcing it, rather than making it less likely to occur in the future. We will talk extensively about this in future chapters.

There Are No Consequences for Misbehavior

Children are well-versed in receiving messages from adults that communicate disapproval about a particular behavior. As parents, we can feel like we're saying "No" or "Don't do that" all day long. However, children learn to tune out the discontented words from adults when consequences are never imposed.

Consider the toddler who is sitting in his high chair eating lunch. You serve him a ham and cheese sandwich. He picks apart the sandwich and begins tossing pieces of ham onto the floor, only eating the cheese and the bread. You say to him, "Don't throw your food on the floor," and proceed to pick up the food and throw it away. He does this repeatedly, although he occasionally pauses in his behavior when you're looking directly at him.

If you were to impart consequences, such as taking away his plate of food (after one or two warnings) or making him get down and pick up the food off the floor each time he threw it, he would be less likely to throw food in the future. Consequences can be powerful teachers.

Variables That Contribute to a Child's Misbehavior

In addition to understanding why children misbehave, it's important to understand that misbehavior does not occur in a vacuum; there are numerous variables that contribute to a child's tendency to misbehave.

Factors That Contribute to a Child's Misbehavior

Child Variables

Child variables are those factors within the child that may influence the child's behavior. These may include:

Fatigue	Personality	Sensory needs
Hunger	Ability to pay attention	Introversion/extroversion
Intelligence	Mood	Ability level for specific task
Emotionality	Coping strategies	Prior experience
Age	Fine/gross motor skills	Language development

Parental Expectations

The expectations of parents and adults may have an influence on the child's behavior. For example, if a parent tolerates a higher level of noise, the child may be more likely to engage in noisy behavior. If a parent has an expectation that homework must be completed before the child can go outside to play, then the child may do this without protest.

This concept is demonstrated when a child acts differently around one parent versus another. Maybe Dad tends to be active, noisy, and more likely to engage in horseplay. In his presence, jumping on the furniture may be permitted. That same behavior, when exhibited in front of Mom, may not be tolerated.

Societal Expectations

Your behavior may change depending on the expectations of the society in which you live. Peer pressure can have a major influence on a child's behavior, for example. If your daughter is playing with a group of social girls who enjoy gossiping about their peers, she may participate, too. In contrast, if she's spending time with only one girl, gossiping may not even be an issue.

When children are in public or in the presence of others, their behavior may reflect the conventions established by the general public rather than those "rules" established in the home environment or when alone. For example, when eating in a restaurant, it's more expected that you will eat using utensils and chew with your mouth closed. When you're by yourself, you may be likely to forgo manners and sit on the couch with your feet up, eating ice cream directly out of the carton.

Environmental Variables

Environmental variables are those factors in the environment or setting that may influence a child's behavior. These may include:

Lighting	Presence of peers	Amount of overall stimulation
Noise level	Presence of adults	Presence of toys/objects in room
Time of day	Freedom of movement	Task demands

Positive Reinforcement, Negative Reinforcement, and Punishment

Legend has it that one evening an old Cherokee told his grandson about a battle that goes on inside people. He said, "My son, the battle is between two wolves inside us all. One is Evil. It is anger, envy, jealousy, sorrow, regret, greed, arrogance, self-pity, guilt, resentment, inferiority, lies, false pride, superiority, and ego. The other is Good. It is joy, peace, love, hope, serenity, humility, kindness, benevolence, empathy, generosity, truth, compassion, and faith." The grandson thought about it for a minute and then asked his grandfather, "Which wolf wins?" The old Cherokee replied, "The one you feed."

This Cherokee legend is relevant to understanding the origins of all behavior.

All behavior stems from reinforcement.
If good behavior is reinforced (fed), then good behavior will be displayed.
If misbehavior is reinforced (fed), then misbehavior will be displayed.

These principles, which originated in 1953 from the work of B. F. Skinner (1953), suggest that as a behavior alters the environment, this behavior can either be positively or negatively reinforced (producing an increase in the frequency of that behavior), or punished (producing at least a temporary decrease in the behavior). Skinner (1969) argued that these concepts impact all of our significant responses in everyday life.

When a particular behavior is initiated, it's intended to meet an internal *need* within the child. Maybe the child needs attention. Maybe the child is trying to connect socially with a peer. Maybe the child is trying to avoid something unpleasant. Regardless, there is a *reason* why the child is behaving this way, even if the child or the parent has difficulty deciphering the underlying need.

Once a behavior is displayed, there is a reaction from the environment. This "environment" may consist of the individuals surrounding the child, the setting, and/or tangible items. Depending on the reaction within the environment, the behavior can be *reinforced* (encouraged or rewarded) or *punished* (strongly discouraged). If the behavior is reinforced, it is much more likely to be repeated.

Let's define the words "reinforcement" (positive and negative) and "punishment," as it can be difficult to recall the difference between "negative reinforcement" and "punishment."

Positive reinforcement is when you add something awesome to the environment in response to a behavior, increasing the likelihood that the behavior will be repeated. Examples include paying someone to mow your lawn, rewarding a child for behaving in the store by giving him ice cream, and showering a child with praise after he works diligently to learn to tie his shoes.

Negative reinforcement increases the likelihood a behavior will be repeated by *taking away* something unpleasant (that's already occurring) from the environment *or* engaging in a positive behavior to completely avoid something unpleasant. Examples include giving a "homework pass" to those students who earn a good grade on an exam, wearing sunscreen to avoid sunburn, or ceasing to nag your spouse when he or she remembers to change the oil in the car every three thousand miles.

Punishment occurs when something *unpleasant is added* to the environment or *something desirable is taken away* after a misbehavior occurs to decrease the likelihood of a behavior recurring. Examples include spanking a child after he runs into the road, assigning chores after a child brings home a poor grade, or placing a toddler in time-out after he hits a peer.

"Internal Needs" Met by Misbehavior

As noted above, all behavior stems from a person's desire to have an *internal need* met. What is an "internal need"? It is the *reason* a child behaves in a certain way. It is the *motivation* behind the behavior. Understanding the internal need of the child assists parents in understanding how best to react to misbehavior.

For example, Daniel is a seven-year-old boy trying to meet an internal need to receive attention from his father. Daniel misbehaves by being disruptive at a restaurant so his father will escort him out to the car, where they will talk casually for several minutes until Daniel's mom and sister finish their meal. Daniel's father could meet his son's need for attention and encourage more socially appropriate behavior by speaking to Daniel throughout the meal, maintaining eye contact, complimenting Daniel when he uses his manners, and ignoring mildly inappropriate behavior.

Six Categories of "Needs"

A review of research indicates that in general, there are six categories of "needs" that motivate people to behave in a particular manner (Jolivette, Barton-Arwood, & Scott, 2000). Everyone experiences each of these needs at any given time, although some needs may be stronger and more frequent than others. The goal is to teach children to attempt to meet these needs in a socially appropriate way rather than via misbehavior.

1. A need for social attention or communication

This need can be described as a desire to connect, either superficially or on a deeper level, with another person or group to receive attention. To meet this need, a child will engage in attention-seeking behavior that may be appropriate, such as telling a funny joke at the lunch table, or inappropriate, such as making fun of the teacher in science class. This need often contributes to a child succumbing to peer pressure. Examples include a child who acts like the class clown and disrupts the class, a girl who gives in to a dare to write her name on the desk in permanent marker, or a boy who brags about his new scooter to a group of peers.

2. Tangible rewards or incentives

This need can be described as a desire to obtain a tangible item, such as a toy, a favorite food, or another coveted object. The fact is, children like "stuff" and will behave in specific ways to obtain it. Examples include a child who earns 20 dollars for each A on his report card, a girl who has a temper outburst to be appeased with a snack in the checkout line, or a boy who helps his mother carry groceries into the house in the hopes of earning more video game time.

3. Escape, avoidance, or delay of tasks

This need can also be described as "avoidance behavior," as its goal is to reduce anxiety or dread about performing a specific task. We all do this at some point or another. Examples include pretending to be ill to avoid giving an oral presentation, watching television instead of doing homework, or hitting the snooze button on the alarm clock instead of getting out of bed.

4. Escape, avoidance, or delay of interaction with specific individuals

Similar to the above need, this need has the goal of reducing anxiety or dread about interacting with a particular individual or group. Examples include a child who has a temper outburst in the waiting room at the dentist's office, a girl who leaves for school before her father wakes up, or a boy who refuses to take the bus because he learns that a bully rides it.

5. Sensory reinforcement

This need can be described as a desire to manage the feedback that our senses (sight, smell, sound, touch, and taste) provide when we interact with our environment. Our behavior may serve to diminish the impact of an overstimulating environment or increase the intensity of an understimulating environment. More specifically, children may fail to meet behavioral demands because they're feeling overwhelmed (they may avoid certain settings or tasks), or they may appear aggressive or impulsive due to a need for more sensory feedback. Examples include a child who has a temper outburst after his mother dresses him in a shirt and tie, a girl who plays aggressively on the playground with her peers, or a boy who vomits after taking a bite of corn.

6. Power, control, or intimidation

This need can be described as a desire to gain dominance over a certain individual or situation. It may stem from the natural expression of a child's strong personality, or it may be a coping strategy to address anxiety or fear. Ideally, this need would manifest itself as "natural leadership ability" rather than bullying or aggression. Examples include a child who insists on being the line leader on the first day of school, a boy who yells at his mother after she directs him to do his chores, or a girl who plays aggressively on the playground with her peers.

As noted above, the goal is to teach children to meet their internal needs in a socially appropriate way, as these needs in and of themselves are valid. It's only when they result in misbehavior that they become problematic.

Each of the example behaviors named above may warrant a different response from the parent, as the *need* is the relevant attribute rather than the actual behavior. Notice that "a girl plays aggressively on the playground with her peers" is an example for both "sensory reinforcement" and "power, control, or intimidation." Although it is the same behavior, the underlying motivation (need) of the child differs. These differing needs require different responses. For example, if the parent would like to meet her daughter's need for sensory stimulation, she may structure playtime so that it consists of more physical activities (jumping on the trampoline or riding bicycles instead of drawing or playing with a toy kitchen set). In contrast, if a parent wants to meet her daughter's need to gain power or control, she may permit her to play with younger children (so that she can be placed in a natural leadership role) or she may structure activities so that her daughter can have a turn deciding upon or facilitating an activity (being the "seeker" in a game of hide and seek, choosing the game, or being placed in charge of passing out the necessary materials). In both of these scenarios, the child's need is acknowledged and met, albeit in a more socially appropriate way.

As another example, Cole may crawl under desks whenever the teacher directs him to read aloud. The function of his behavior may be to escape embarrassment, as he is convinced that he cannot read well enough to avoid teasing from his more able peers. The next step is to design positive interventions that will reduce his likelihood of feeling embarrassed but will not result in misbehavior. For example, the teacher may propose that Cole does not have to read aloud unless he raises his hand to volunteer. Also, the teacher may implement an academically based intervention in hopes of improving Cole's reading skills and consequently improving his self-confidence.

Examining the Whole Child

"He's too sensitive."

"She's so emotional."

"He just wants what he wants when he wants it."

After uttering these phrases, the parents will request that their child be made to be less tenderhearted, calmer, or more likely to listen. Instead, parents would benefit from examining the factors that contribute to their child's displaying oversensitivity, emotionality, or poor listening skills. Although the child may have a natural propensity toward these characteristics, it is likely that outside variables have reinforced them.

Namely, parents must investigate the *Whole Child*, or all the factors that contribute to a child's behavioral success or failure.

The Whole Child

All too often, parents do not take into account all of the factors that influence behavior. When parents overlook crucial components, they may be setting the stage for failure, creating or contributing to an environment that will inevitably lead to misbehavior. It's helpful to first consider physical aspects of the child—namely sleep, nutrition, and sensory issues—when trying to prevent misbehavior.

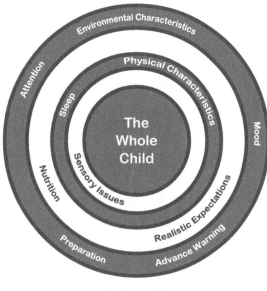

The Whole Child

Sleep

Many people do not realize the true importance of sleep until they have an infant whose care drastically impacts their ability to get several hours of uninterrupted sleep each night. Suddenly, concentrating well enough to drive the car in a straight line seems difficult. Remembering three items needed at the grocery store seems taxing. A normally cheerful demeanor may become one of extreme testiness, mild anxiety, and quick tears.

Children, it turns out, are not so different when faced with sleep deprivation. All aspects of children's functioning—including behavior, physical development, emotional adjustment, mood, and the ability to learn and problem-solve—are impacted by sleep. According to the National Sleep Foundation (www.sleepfoundation.org), up to 40 percent of childhood is spent sleeping. However, chronic sleep deprivation in children (and adults) is becoming an epidemic in our society. Research indicates that across all age groups, children are sleeping an average of one hour less per night than children from a century ago (Matricciani, Olds & Petkov, 2012). In adolescence, the amount of sleep that a child gets each night is greatly reduced by social factors, such as the demands placed on them by school and extracurricular activities, the prevalence of caffeine in their diet, and excessive use of technology and media.

Characteristic	How Sleep Impacts This Characteristic
Obesity	Short sleep duration is a risk factor for obesity for these potential reasons: • Hormonal and metabolic changes that result in increased hunger and appetite • Increased fatigue and reduced physical activity • Poor decision making with regard to food choices • Increased awake time in which to eat It should be noted that these results are more prevalent in children younger than 12 years old and cannot be consistently found in research studies involving adults.
Symptoms typically associated with a diagnosis of ADHD	Children with sleep disturbances are more likely to display symptoms such as impaired attention and concentration, increased hyperactivity, poor memory, and impaired planning ability.
Emotional response/coping strategies	Sleep deprivation has been shown to negatively impact children's ability to adapt to challenging situations. In addition, children are unable to take full advantage of positive experiences.
Motor skills (fine and gross)	Sleep deprivation has been associated with less well developed motor skills, both fine and gross.

(continued)

Academic performance	Sleep deprivation has been associated with lower academic performance and depressed IQ scores.
Drug and alcohol use	Children with sleep disturbances are more likely to experience chronic difficulties with drug and alcohol use in adolescence and adulthood.
Internalizing behavior	Children with sleep disturbances display frequent and more severe symptoms of anxiety and depression.
Externalizing behavior	Children with sleep disturbances display more frequent and more severe externalizing behaviors, including aggression, hyperactivity, and defiance.

As indicated in the table above, sleep disturbances are associated with numerous difficulties, including obesity, characteristics typically associated with ADHD, poor coping strategies, less well developed motor skills, lower academic performance, increased likelihood to abuse drugs and alcohol as adults, increased symptoms of anxiety and depression, and increased aggressive and defiant behavior.

It should be noted that researchers continue to debate the causal relationship between sleep and these variables. More specifically, does a lack of sleep result in more frequent diagnoses of ADHD, or does the presence of ADHD impact a child's ability to sleep? Continued research is necessary. However, it's universally agreed that parents need to prioritize and protect children's sleep in order to assist them in developing long-term, healthy sleep habits and to increase the likelihood of their success in all areas of life.

Although the amount of sleep that a child needs to optimize their performance is somewhat individualized, there are some general guidelines to follow when planning your child's schedule (see the table below). While children cannot be *forced* to sleep, parents can certainly structure a child's environment and schedule to maximize exposure to ideal sleeping conditions. Parents often allot too little of their child's day to sleeping time and therefore do not have a true understanding of their child's sleeping needs.

Age	Amount of Time Per Day That Should Be Spent Sleeping (Including Naps)
Birth to 4 months	Up to 18 hours
4 months to 1 year	14 to 15 hours
1 year to 3 years	12 to 14 hours
3 years to 5 years	10 to 12 hours
6 years to 12 years	10 to 11 hours
Adolescence	8 to 10 hours
Adulthood	7 to 9 hours

Tips for Developing Healthy Sleep Habits in Children

1. **Establish consistent awake and sleep times, including nap times.**

   Often parents express that one of the most frustrating aspects of parenting small children is how schedule-driven they are; parents may feel held hostage by the physical needs of their children. However, children benefit from a schedule, particularly with regard to sleep and nutrition. By the age of four months, children should be encouraged to maintain a consistent sleep schedule that includes being placed in a crib in a quiet, darkened room at the same time every day. Parents who regularly skip naptime or fail to provide adequate sleeping conditions are increasing their child's sleep debt (accumulated hours of sleep that are lost to other factors, such as illness or environment), which greatly increases the likelihood that their child will exhibit misbehavior that's more frequent and/or severe. Vacation, illness, and holiday events often lead to a change in sleeping routine, yet it is during these times that parents would most appreciate good behavior. Therefore, parents should prioritize their child's sleep times as much as possible, even when it's difficult to do so.

2. **Establish consistent "pre-sleep" routines.**

   Children benefit from routine, as routines provide cues about what to expect in the near future. Children will have an easier time falling asleep quickly and without tears if there is a series of comforting, predictable behaviors that occur immediately prior to sleep time. For infants, a bedtime routine is likely to consist of a bath, diaper change, feeding, and lullaby/story time, after which the baby is placed in her crib awake but drowsy. For an older child, a typical routine may consist of a bath, pajamas, teeth brushing, and story time. Similar good-night phrases may be uttered each night, such as "Sweet dreams. I love you. I'll see you in the morning." It is soothing to repeat these exact words with a sweet and loving lilt in your voice. Perhaps you'll hear back "Love you too!" Little variation is encouraged, even when the child is ill or sleeping away from home.

3. **Encourage independence.**

   Research indicates that children who are taught to fall asleep independently and self-soothe after waking in the night and during naps have fewer nighttime awakenings and less fussiness after naptime (Hall, Scher, Zaidman-Zait, Espezel & Warnock,

2012). When parents are too involved in a child's experience in falling asleep, they may compromise the child's ability to develop healthy coping strategies to deal with natural variations in the sleep cycle. Being able to self-soothe and self-regulate during sleep times helps a child to develop effective emotional coping strategies when confronted with challenging or frustrating situations. Therefore, parents should teach their children to fall asleep without the presence of a parent or television.

Nutrition

All of us, adults and children alike, struggle with emotional regulation when experiencing hunger or thirst. Irritability runs rampant, problem-solving skills take a nosedive, and it's difficult to enjoy even pleasurable activities. Not receiving adequate nourishment at regular intervals can negatively impact a child's behavioral and emotional development.

While there is extensive research on best practices in nutrition with regard to the benefits of eating organic and the impact of food allergies, hormones, gluten, sugar, and additives, this book instead focuses on specific, concrete suggestions that a parent can use to encourage healthy eating habits.

Tips for Developing Healthy Eating Habits in Children

1. Provide three balanced meals per day.

The United States Department of Agriculture Center of Nutrition Policy and Promotion endorses the concept of "My Plate," rather than the more traditional food pyramid, to illustrate a balanced and proportional meal.

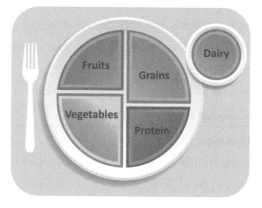

My Plate

Parents should attempt to provide three balanced meals per day that consist of a protein, fruit, grain, vegetable, and dairy. A sample of three simple meals may consist of:

- *Breakfast*: an egg with a slice of tomato, a slice of whole-wheat toast, half of a banana, and a small glass of milk
- *Lunch*: a ham and cheese sandwich on whole-wheat bread, baby carrots, grapes, and either a small glass of milk or some yogurt
- *Dinner*: chicken, brown rice, green beans, pineapple, and a small glass of milk

It should be acknowledged that it is unrealistic to expect all children to *actually* consume three well-balanced meals per day, given their likelihood to eschew vegetables or new foods, have a variable appetite, and get distracted while eating. The goal should simply be to *expose* the child to three balanced meals per day.

2. Respect your meal times.

In general, meal times should occur at approximately the same time each day. This provides a consistent provision of nutrients and energy. Parents should also avoid feeding a large meal to children right before bedtime, as it may stimulate the child's digestive system to the point where falling asleep is more difficult.

3. Limit snacking.

Parents often complain that their children are poor eaters who refuse to try new foods, avoid vegetables, and prefer to "graze" on snack foods throughout the day rather than partake of three full meals and one or two snacks. Despite parents' best efforts, snack foods are typically less nutritious and often lead to diminished consumption of all the necessary food groups. This habit of perpetually snacking is one that will only continue if parents permit it. If three balanced meals are provided at consistent intervals throughout the day, one midmorning and one midafternoon snack should suffice.

4. Sit while eating.

Your child should be encouraged to eat mindfully. Sitting in a chair, preferably at a table (not on the couch or in the car), is a great way to encourage conscious eating. In addition, this provides parents with the opportunity to teach manners, facilitate conversation, and role-model their own eating habits to their children.

5. **Limit food and drinks that contain caffeine.**

   Caffeine is a stimulant that can negatively impact your child's ability to fall asleep at naptime or nighttime. In addition, most food and drinks that contain caffeine, such as soda, iced tea, energy drinks, and chocolate, are unhealthy or have little nutritional value. It is best to avoid them.

6. **Avoid power struggles with regard to food and/or meal times.**

   One of the most common concerns voiced by parents is that their child "refuses to eat." Here are some things to remember:

   • Children cannot be forced to eat.

   • Children will eat when they are hungry.

   • Children will not develop an appreciation for foods to which they are not exposed.

   • Children are likely to pattern their food consumption after that of their role models.

   • Most children find that provoking an emotional response in their parent with regard to food is rewarding. Provoking a negative response is just as rewarding as provoking a positive response.

   In order to avoid or minimize power struggles at the dinner table:

   • Avoid trying to force your children to eat. Simply require them to remain seated at the table for at least 15 minutes during meal times. Encourage them to eat with one or two positively worded prompts, but don't punish them for not eating. (However, feel free to offer consequences for misbehavior such as using poor manners, doing unappetizing things with their food, or whining/complaining.)

   • Increase the likelihood of your children having an appetite at mealtimes by avoiding excessive snacking and offering at least one or two food items they have previously consumed.

   • Offer a balanced meal at each mealtime, even if it consists of food that you suspect your children will not enjoy. In order to earn dessert or a snack later, they must try at least one bite (a "polite bite") of each undesired food item. Many parents find the "one bite per year" to be a helpful rule (e.g., "You're four years old, so you must eat four bites").

- Role-model appropriate eating behaviors. Eat the same food you'd like your children to eat, sit at the table for at least 15 minutes, use good manners, and speak positively about the food offered.

- If your children choose not to eat, simply respect their decision after encouraging them to eat in a positive tone one to three times. For example, a parent might say, "Mmm…I like these peas with a little butter on them. Try a bite and tell me what you think." Avoid using emotionally laden words such as "Mommy will be so disappointed if you don't try her casserole" and matter-of-factly state the consequences: "If you're not going to eat, please ask to be excused and carry your dish to the counter. Our next meal is at six o'clock, and there will be no snacks between now and then." Keep the conversation focused on topics unrelated to your child's eating behavior and briefly praise him or her for using manners and eating well.

Note: These concepts only apply to typically developing children. Consult your physician if your child has a medical condition that interferes with appetite or the processing of food, experiences significant emotional symptoms, has a severe sensory response, or if you have a reason to believe that your child is suffering from Reactive Attachment Disorder.

Sensory Issues

Lila, a friendly four-year-old, was invited to a friend's birthday party. She was initially excited to learn that it would be hosted at a noisy, brightly lit place filled with bounce houses and slides. However, when she arrived, Lila clutched her mother's hand and refused to participate. Throughout the entire birthday party, Lila remained withdrawn and didn't even have a slice of cake or sing happy birthday. She didn't necessarily appear unhappy, but she clearly didn't want to participate. Lila's mom was frustrated and puzzled.

All of us respond to the feedback that our senses (sight, smell, sound, touch, and taste) provide when we interact with our environment. However, depending on the individual, the nature and intensity of our response varies. If our response is too intense, we may feel uncomfortable and overwhelmed by our environment. If our response is not intense enough, we may feel understimulated and unsatisfied and crave more sensory feedback.

Misbehavior can result from an incompatibility between our senses and our environment. Some children are *overreactors*—they are sensitive to the stimuli in our environment and experience sensations more strongly than the typical person. This may cause them to withdraw from stimuli in an attempt to control their intensity. Lila, in the above example, is one such child.

Think of the child who hates noise and chaos. He shies away from big groups of people. He gets tearful or quickly tattles when a peer is playing too roughly. He may be ticklish, hate strong-tasting foods or foods with unusual textures, and get irritable if he's out in the sun too long or if he gets dirty, wet, or cold. His mood, attention, problem-solving ability, and ability to self-soothe may be severely impacted when he feels overwhelmed. This child, because of his sensitivity, may appear defensive, resistant, stubborn, and withdrawn.

In contrast, other children are *underreactors*—their brain doesn't register sensory information efficiently, and they miss many sensory cues. As a consequence, these children may actively seek sensory input in order to accumulate enough sensory information to feel adequately stimulated.

Think of the child who enjoys playing aggressively. He may run too fast for the space allotted. He may enjoy crashing into objects and other people. He may talk too loudly, constantly put things in his mouth, throw things, hop and jump instead of walk, and appear relatively immune to being dirty, cold, or wet. He's a boy who underreacts—fails to register information—to his environment; he needs to manufacture an intense response in order to feel physically satisfied with the environment. However, this need for increased stimulation can cause him to get in trouble constantly, as he may be viewed as overactive, aggressive, impulsive, a poor listener, and callous to other people's feelings and personal space.

Sensory issues are oftentimes associated with children with atypical development, such as those diagnosed with Autism Spectrum Disorder, Attention-Deficit Hyperactivity Disorder (ADHD), or Sensory Integration Disorder. These children may have a more severe sensory response to their environment and may require significant interventions to improve their functioning in their day-to-day setting. If your child's sensory issues are impacting his or her ability to participate in crucial activities (eating, sleeping, playing, or socializing even in calm settings), it is recommended that you consult your doctor, who may refer you to a professional specializing in sensory integration, such as an occupational therapist.

However, unbeknownst to most parents, most children exhibit at least mild sensory issues in at least one domain, such as response to noise, light, textures, touch, or smell.

These sensory reactions most assuredly contribute to their behavior. Understanding your child's individual response to sensory information can be an effective tool in setting the stage for behavioral success.

> **True Tale**
>
> I learned about my son's sensory issues, particularly with regard to noise and feeling crowded, when he was about 18 months old. He screamed relentlessly when I brought him to a busy food court at the mall. Finally, I left to walk him to the car. Upon exiting the mall, his tears stopped immediately. From that point on, I have always been mindful about asking him to participate in activities that are excessively noisy.

When your child is behaving in an undesirable manner, it's important that you consider whether his or her behavior is simply a result of a sensory issue rather than true "misbehavior," as it may greatly influence how you respond.

Tips for Supporting Your Child with Mild Sensory Issues

1. **Avoid nonessential settings that will trigger an unpleasant sensory response.**
    While there are many environments that a child cannot avoid, such as the busy cafeteria in an elementary school or a dentist's office, there are just as many settings that you can avoid if you know they are going to wreak havoc on your child's senses. For example, taking your child to see a movie when you know she's sensitive to loud noises and darkness is unnecessary. Similarly, it's unfair to expect your child to play football aggressively when he's easily upset by being bumped into and crowded into a huddle. Be mindful of these situations and prioritize essential activities.

2. **Provide advance warning when the environment is expected to be incompatible with your child's sensory needs.**
    Children are more likely to tolerate an incompatible environment if they've been given advance warning about what to expect. My son, sensitive to noise, greatly benefits from being told, "During the parade there's going to be loud music and the sound of horns. You can cover your ears if it gets too loud." Advance warning allows the child to mentally prepare for the upcoming activity, increasing the likelihood that he can participate successfully.

3. **Provide accommodations whenever possible.**

Sometimes parents can provide accommodations to minimize the impact that an incompatible sensory environment can have on a child. This is particularly helpful for overreactors, as these children find sensory information to be overwhelming. For example, the following accommodations may be helpful:

- Bring earplugs to mute loud noises.
- Use headphones to drown out unpleasant sounds with appealing music.
- Pack a lunch to replace food that they find unappealing in taste or texture.
- Let them choose their own clothes to minimize complaints about the presence of tags or a poor fit.
- Encourage them to wear sunglasses and/or a hat to block out bright light.
- Avoid overheating.
- Bring a change of clothes in case they get wet or excessively dirty.

For an underreactor, in contrast, it may be necessary to provide your child with additional opportunities for physical stimulation, such as increased time playing outside, tumbling, dancing or swinging; enrolling her in sports activities; and increasing tactile stimulation through the use of Play-Doh®, sand, or water.

4. **Practice ... in small doses.**

Mild sensory issues are likely to be alleviated over time, particularly if parents consistently and gradually expose their child to all kinds of sensory stimulation at a rate that their child can tolerate. For example, a child who is sensitive to food textures may be offered yogurt with chunks of fruit in it several days per week. A child who dislikes loud noises may be gifted with a super fun toy that's noisy. A child who hates having her hair brushed may allow you to finger-comb it initially.

Final Thoughts

Many parenting books offer specific strategies to be used with specific misbehavior. While there will be a place in this book for such suggestions, I want to encourage parents to adopt a specific problem-solving strategy to deal with misbehavior.

Understanding why children misbehave, the factors that influence misbehavior, and the motivation behind misbehavior is necessary to prevent and respond to misbehavior with mindfulness and efficiency.

Key Points Discussed in Chapter 2

- There is motivation behind nearly all behavior. Shaping behavior is dependent upon understanding this motivation.

- There are numerous variables that contribute to misbehavior in children. Among them are those specific to the child and those related to the environment, the society in which we live, and parental expectations.

- People are driven by a desire to meet an internal need. The behavior that is produced from the attempt to meet these needs is the direct result of reinforcement. Therefore, a parent's goal is to teach the child to meet his or her internal needs in a socially acceptable manner by reinforcing positive behavior.

- A review of research indicates that there are six general categories of "needs" that drive behavior: social attention/communication, tangible rewards, escape/avoidance of tasks, escape/avoidance of interaction with specific people, sensory reinforcement, or power/control. Understanding the need of the child can guide parents in how to teach and reinforce positive behavior.

- The Whole Child should be examined when assessing misbehavior. The Whole Child consists of both external, parent-influenced variables (advance warning, attention, preparation, realistic behavioral expectations, and mood) and internal, physiological variables (sleep, nutrition, and sensory needs). Understanding these variables can make parents feel empowered and more in control, as they are variables that can be manipulated to best meet the child's needs.

- One of the most basic interventions for misbehavior is to improve the length and quality of a child's sleep. Although parents cannot force a child to sleep, they can structure their child's environment and schedule to maximize their child's exposure to ideal sleeping conditions, hopefully eliciting better-quality sleep.

- Poor nutrition and eating habits can contribute to misbehavior. Parents can establish structured mealtimes and avoid power struggles at the dinner table.

- How we respond to sensory information (sight, smell, sound, touch, and taste) varies by individual, and most children exhibit at least mild sensory issues in at least one domain. Some children overreact to their environment (they experience sensations more strongly than the typical person), while others underreact to their environment (their brain doesn't register sensory information efficiently, and they actively seek sensory input to become adequately stimulated). Addressing your child's sensory needs can help set the stage for behavioral success.

Chapter 3

Empowering Parents

Many of the parents with whom I work seem to feel as though every day is a parenting mystery. They keep their fingers crossed in hopes that their children will have a good day; a day when they listen, comply, and remain free of temper outbursts. Parents are unable to appreciate that they have a considerable influence over how their child responds throughout the day. They have the opportunity to "set the stage" for good behavior. I call this "preventative parenting." This is when parents use mindful, proactive strategies in order to prevent a child from beginning the downward spiral that results in significant misbehavior.

In contrast to Chapter 2, a portion of which focused on internal physiological factors that impact the Whole Child, the goal of this chapter is to discuss the ways in which parents can set the stage for good behavior and increase their awareness of their ability to shape their child's behavior. Specifically, we're going to discuss the benefits of advance warnings, attention, preparation, realistic expectations, and parental mood and attitude.

True Tale

When my daughter first began attending kindergarten, I learned that she had daily home assignments. In a quest to develop good homework habits, I initially insisted that she complete these brief assignments immediately upon her arrival home. After a series of irritable outbursts and poor adherence to directions, I learned that it was unrealistic to expect her to attend to academic tasks without a period of play and relaxation. In addition, I learned that she greatly benefitted from advance notice prior to switching gears from play time to homework. Once I learned to "set the stage" for good behavior based on her needs, our afternoons proceeded more smoothly.

Transitions and Advance Warning

Elaine, the mother of a three-year-old boy named Robert, expresses frustration with her son's inability to "listen to me when I tell him to do something, even if it's something that he normally finds to be fun or rewarding." She describes incidences when Robert won't allow her to put on his shoes even though they are leaving for his music class, won't put on his bathing suit despite his love of swimming, or will not leave a playdate even though he's expressed that he's tired of spending time with a specific peer. Elaine reports that his refusal behavior often results in her scolding him, physically assisting him in getting dressed or moving from one location to another, and generally making every interaction seem difficult. After a thorough discussion, it becomes apparent that Robert is a child who struggles to make transitions.

Let's stop and think for a minute. When you're in the middle of watching a television program, do you like it when your spouse enters the room and turns off the television without warning? When you're sleeping, do you welcome the idea of transitioning from a restful sleep to leaving your bed when only given a minute to do so? At work, do you prefer to go from one meeting to the next without a break in between? Gearing up mentally for the next activity in your day is essential to maintaining a calm attitude and effective problem-solving skills. In addition, adults use planners, warning alerts on their smartphones, reminders from administrative staff, and written cues such as memos, text messages, and e-mails to remember our routines and provide us with advance warnings of upcoming events.

In contrast, many parents simply expect their children to transition to the next activity with little more than a verbal prompt provided moments before the desired transition. And unless every day looks the same (unlikely), children aren't necessarily able to make accurate predictions as to what will occur next and adjust their behavior accordingly.

Types of Transitions

There are two basic types of transitions:

1. *Long-term transition:* transitions that are lengthy and relatively gradual, such as the birth of a new sibling, a separation or divorce, a move, or the beginning or end of a school year. These types of transitions tend to be infrequent but may significantly disrupt a child's routine or current way of life. They have the potential to trigger misbehavior that is mild, such as whining or a temporary increase in temper

outbursts, or relatively severe, such as significant eating or sleeping disturbances, separation anxiety, sadness or withdrawal, or chronic mild or severe aggression.

2. *Short-term transition:* the transition from one daily activity to the next, such as transitioning from eating breakfast to getting dressed, leaving a playdate to go home for dinner, or turning off the television to get ready for bed. These types of transitions happen dozens of times throughout the day and have the potential to trigger misbehavior that is relatively minor (dawdling, feigning helplessness) or more troublesome (temper outbursts, aggression, or outright refusal).

Children need to be given advance warning in order to physically and emotionally prepare for a transition to a new activity.

Tips for Giving Advance Warning and Setting Clear Expectations

1. Describe the next (or future) activity clearly and concisely. Tell the child what the activity will consist of and what it will look like.
2. Tell them *when* the activity is likely to occur.
3. Tell them the behavior that is *expected* of them during the activity.
4. Clearly describe what *consequences* will occur if they don't meet the behavioral expectations.
5. Adhere to the consequences each time.

Scenario 1

Mom: Tomorrow we're going to wake up, get dressed and eat breakfast, then go to Grandma's house to go swimming. We need to bring our bathing suits and towels. While we're there, you will need to wear your life vest.

Danny: I don't want to wear my life vest! I never have to when we go swimming at our pool.

Mom: I know, but Grandma's pool is much deeper, and I'm going to need to watch your sister too. If you don't wear your life vest, you won't be allowed to go swimming.

Danny: I don't want to wear it, Mom!

Mom: I know. It's disappointing, but if you make a fuss about wearing it, you will have to sit in a chair at the side of the pool while your sister swims, or we will simply go home. You must wear the life vest the entire time we are there. Do you understand?

Danny (sulkily): Yes, I understand.

In the above scenario, Mom clearly describes where they are going, when, the behavior expected, and the consequences that will result if the expectations are unmet. In addition, she validates Danny's feelings when he protests (yet continues to maintain her expectations) and checks for comprehension to ensure that he understands what's expected, even though he's agitated.

Scenario 2

Dad: After we finish grocery shopping, we're going to stop at the sandwich place and eat some dinner. While we're in the restaurant, I need you to stay in your seats and speak in a quiet voice. If you cannot do this, we will leave your food behind and come home.

Similar to Scenario 1, Dad describes the transition (*finish shopping and go to a restaurant*), notes when it will happen (*after shopping*), clearly outlines the desired behavior (*stay in your seats and speak quietly*), and states the consequences if the expectations are unmet (*leave food behind and come home*).

Scenario 3

Mom: In two minutes, I'd like you to start cleaning up all the toys in the playroom. After you do so, we can pick out the movie we want to watch for movie night. We can't start the movie until all the toys are put away.

Children: Okay.

(Five minutes later.)

Mom: You haven't started picking up the toys. If all the toys are not picked up in the next 10 minutes, we're not going to have time to watch the movie before bedtime. We'll have to do movie night another night. Do you understand?

Children: Yes.

Mom: Can you explain to me what I just said?

Children: If we don't pick up the toys, we can't watch a movie.

(Ten minutes go by.)

Mom: Because the toys haven't been cleaned up like I asked, we won't have time for a movie tonight.

Children: Awww, c'mon! That's not fair!

Mom: Your choices are to pick up the toys or go to bed right away. But we won't have time to watch a movie tonight.

In this final scenario, Mom clearly adheres to the "tips" described previously in this chapter. In addition, this example illustrates how Mom follows through with the consequences described. The result of giving an advance warning of consequences is that (hopefully) your child will understand that that these consequences are the direct result of *his* poor choices, rather than *your* being punitive.

Attention

Parents are among the busiest people in our society. In addition to managing their own lives, they have to teach, nurture, plan for, and protect their children. This requires organizational ability and patience, two qualities that can be in short supply when trying to take care of adult responsibilities while caring for your child.

As any parent who has ever tried to have a phone conversation lasting longer than five minutes can attest, misbehavior often occurs when a child senses that their parent is distracted or inattentive. Most parents learn this the hard way—my son once tied several scarves together and attempted to swing from the stairs to the couch while I was trying to purchase online movie tickets for the latest movie.

The first question parents should ask themselves when their child is actively misbehaving is "Have I been attending to my child enough?"

Children cannot be attended to every moment of the day. In fact, they *shouldn't* be attended to every moment of the day. Please note that "attend" is defined as "actively engaged with." They need to learn to entertain themselves, discover how to structure their own time and activities, and experience the consequences of their decision making. Children won't develop these skills magically; the skills need to be taught and practiced from a young age. While children who are 12 months old may be able to entertain themselves for only a few minutes, children should become increasingly independent as they get older.

Crucial point: Provide attention (and praise) while your child is behaving appropriately.

However, children benefit from intermittent attention—attention that is distributed frequently and randomly in short bursts. For example, if you need to complete several household chores on a Saturday morning, it may be tempting to explain to your children that you need two uninterrupted hours to work, then you'll all do something fun as a family.

Instead, set aside three (instead of two) hours for your chores. Stop working every 20 or 30 minutes (depending on the age of your child or how long it takes for your house to get eerily quiet as your child is making plans to put makeup on the dog or swallow all the pennies that were found in the dryer). Seek out your child and initiate a short, pleasurable activity with them *while they are still behaving*. It may be playing a quick game of Uno. It may be admiring their latest trick on their skateboard. It may be tickling them on their bed and listening to their favorite song. But two or three moments of attention can prevent misbehavior that could result in the entire day being ruined. This will reinforce their positive behavior. If you only provide attention while they are misbehaving, you are simply increasing the likelihood that the misbehavior will occur again.

Remember, bored children = naughty children.

Be Prepared

Dan, father to Noah, age 14 months, once boarded a plane armed with only a bottle of formula, a receiving blanket, his cell phone, and his car keys. Approximately 20 minutes into the 90-minute flight, Noah soiled his diaper in the messiest manner possible. By the end of the flight, Noah was naked from the waist down, wrapped in his receiving blanket, and sucking on his father's dirty keys after he had tossed dad's cell phone on the floor. The matronly woman next to him, her tone oozing disapproval, leaned over to him and stated the obvious: "You should have come more prepared."

Needless to say, stating the obvious wasn't very helpful in this situation.

Tips for Being Prepared

1. Consider your child's physical needs.

When preparing for an activity, it's helpful to factor in the need for drinks, snacks, meals, and bathroom breaks. You may also need to plan for a break in activity to rest or take a nap. Finally, factor in clothing choices—weather and temperature need to be considered, as well as the nature of the activity (a change of clothes if they get wet or dirty, or sneakers if they'll be active, for example).

2. **Consider the length of time and the entertainment value of the activity.**

In addition to factoring in physical needs, parents must be prepared with the appropriate materials to ensure that the child is entertained for the appropriate length of time. For example, bringing a coloring book and a handful of crayons to a pediatrician's appointment when you know the pediatrician typically runs 45 minutes late is insufficient. Instead, consider packing a small backpack full of activities. Many activities aren't inherently entertaining (such as going to the movies or playing at the park), and parents can prevent misbehavior when they have materials to occupy their children. Most importantly, recognize that you may have to remain engaged with your child for a significant portion of the wait, rather than simply sitting complacently while he plays alongside you.

Realistic Behavioral Expectations

Setting realistic behavioral expectations involves considering all of the factors already addressed in this chapter, as well as your child's developmental stage, your priorities, and your child's skills and ability level.

Expecting your child to participate cheerfully at a birthday party that involves riding a pony may be unrealistic if your child has always expressed fear around large animals. Expecting your three-year-old to successfully nap while you are sharing a room on vacation with their noisy, rambunctious older cousin is unreasonable. Expecting your five-year-old to remain seated in a waiting room for an hour without age-appropriate stimulation is impractical. In fact, expecting your child to engage in these activities successfully, without considerable intervention by you, is setting them up for failure.

Factors to Consider When Setting Realistic Behavioral Expectations

1. Factor in your child's developmental stage.

Dana, mother to Jesse, age two-and-a-half, took her son to her niece's birthday party. Jesse happily participated in a series of activities that included using sidewalk chalk, blowing bubbles, running through the sprinkler, and singing "Happy Birthday" to the birthday girl. When it came time to open presents, Jesse pushed to the front of the group and began "helping" his cousin open up a series of colorful, exciting gifts. Dana quickly urged Jesse to step away, reminding him that the gifts were not for him. He began crying and attempting to reach the gifts, eventually engaging in a noisy, disruptive temper outburst. Frustrated and embarrassed,

Dana removed him from the room, scolded him, and demanded that he apologize to the birth-day girl after he calmed down. Although he eventually apologized, it was apparent that he didn't understand why he was doing so.

In this scenario, the fact that Jesse desired to be involved in the gift-opening portion of the party is age-appropriate. It is, after all, difficult for a two-year-old child to suspend a desire for instant gratification and understand that there are times when he receives gifts, and there are times when he's simply a spectator. Rather than acknowledging that Jesse's outburst resulted from his being developmentally unable to understand a more mature concept, his mother simply regarded it as misbehavior. Being more mindful of his developmental needs may have resulted in Dana treating this as an opportunity to start to educate Jesse on the social skills involved in attending a birthday party, rather than viewing it as an embarrassing example of misbehavior. Even better, she could have used an advance warning to prepare Jesse for the inevitable gift-opening portion of the party.

2. Prioritize.

Allison, mother to Bryce, woke up every morning dreading the inevitable battle that occurred while getting him ready for kindergarten. Each morning, Allison would lay out Bryce's clothing for school—jeans, a polo shirt, underwear, and athletic socks. Each morning, Bryce would don the underwear and balk at the remainder of his mother's choices. Oftentimes, he'd come down to breakfast wearing athletic shorts, a T-shirt, and sneakers without socks, which Allison felt looked sloppy.

After months of this daily struggle, Allison consulted a professional. Within moments, she was confronted with the question, "Does Bryce's school permit him to wear athletic shorts, a T-shirt, and sneakers without socks?" She answered yes. The follow-up question was, "Why does it matter to you what he wears if he's comfortable and tantrum-free?" In this situation, it was helpful to discuss whether the clothing preferred by Allison was truly necessary based on the expectations of the school or simply a personal preference that, upon reflection, could be abandoned for the sake of fostering harmony. After all, sometimes parents are quick to classify a child's

> **Keep in mind that prioritizing behavioral expectations doesn't simply mean lowering your behavioral expectations.**

refusal to indulge our arbitrary preferences as a behavior issue, rather than recognize that it may be more functional to just let it go. It's important that parents' behavioral expectations be child-focused, rather than an extension of our fears that we may not have a "perfect" child or demonstrate "perfect" parenting skills.

Prioritize

After much discussion, Allison and Bryce agreed that he could wear the clothes he preferred as long as they were clean, matching, and fit well. This compromise resulted in mornings that were less drama-filled. Oftentimes, if children are strong-willed or if parents have set a poor precedent for discipline in the past, parents simply lower their expectations to avoid conflict. For example, rather than insisting that our child remain seated and use their manners during meals, we simply allow him or her to grab food off the table and wander around, as long as he or she is not bothering other diners. Or, instead of insisting that our young child share toys with peers, we simply appeal to the older child with words such as, "Please, Peyton? Can't Caleb take another turn? He doesn't understand how to share as well as you do yet, but maybe he'll learn by watching you." Although this may temporarily deescalate the situation, it certainly isn't a long-term solution.

Decide which behavioral expectations are the most important to you in any given situation for your particular child. Is it that your child display manners? Refrain from having a temper outburst? Follow the teacher's directions? Prioritize your expectations, and factor in your child's age and ability level. Once you determine these expectations, send a consistent message about them to your child. Don't complicate things by discussing five different behavioral expectations when only two of them really matter to you.

> **Parents, pick your battles.**

3. Factor in skill deficit versus performance deficit.

When a child fails to display a desirable behavior, parents often make statements like "He's too stubborn to behave in a restaurant," or "She refuses to wait her turn," or "He won't listen to the teacher." The implication is that the child *knows* how to engage in the behavior, but is simply choosing not to.

This is where the concepts of *skill deficit* versus *performance deficit* come into play.

> A *skill deficit* is when a child cannot display the behavior. The child doesn't know how.
>
> A *performance deficit* is when a child can display the behavior but does not.

Parents must ask themselves, "Does my child know how to engage in this behavior?" More specifically, they need to decide if the child knows how to engage in the positive behavior *consistently* and *in the setting(s) in which it is expected*.

Just because you've seen your child sit patiently once or twice during story time at the library does not mean that this is a skill that is well-developed enough to be displayed across all settings. After all, sitting patiently during a high-interest activity (story time) is easier than sitting patiently during a low-interest activity (a church sermon or in a shopping cart in a stagnant line). To feel certain that your child has the ability to successfully engage in the positive behavior, you must have observed them doing so on a consistent basis (at least five times or more within a relatively short period of time) and be realistic about whether this skill is likely to be displayed in a particular setting. Once a parent determines that a child is lacking the skill to behave in a specific manner, the parent needs to focus on *teaching* the child that behavior.

If there is a *skill deficit*, the child needs to be *taught* the positive behavior. If there is a *performance deficit*, the child needs to be *motivated* to do the desired behavior.

Remember:

Good behavior has to be taught.

Good behavior has to be role-modeled.

Good behavior has to be reinforced.

Often.

Specific strategies on how to "teach" or reinforce positive behavior are discussed in Chapter 4, but in general, remember role-modeling positive behavior is an effective teaching tool.

Mood/Attitude

Last Saturday, Lisa's husband was working and she was spending time with her two boys, ages six and eight. It was an extremely hot summer day, and Lisa wanted the time she spent with her boys to be fun and exciting. After asking them to help choose an activity, they decided upon going to a nearby amusement park. Lisa thought, "The temperature is in the mid-90s today. It's going to be so hot. I hate walking around in the sun in such high temperatures." But rather than voicing her concerns, Lisa headed to the amusement park with her family. Within an hour of arriving, Lisa was hot, sweaty, and grouchy. She snapped at her sons for laughing too loudly on several occasions, felt resentful that she needed to spend ten dollars on cold drinks, and generally felt irritable and exhausted. She just wanted to go home, and despite her efforts to hide her bad mood, the boys detected it. The day was spoiled.

Everyone would have been better off had Lisa shared her dread of walking around in the extreme heat and helped choose an equally appealing indoor activity. When it comes to "setting the stage," it may be helpful to factor in the parent's current mood and attitude, within reason. For example, it may not be a good idea to have a playdate with three of the noisiest neighborhood kids on the day after Mom was kept up all night with an ailing two-year-old.

Part of parenting is taking advantage of all learning opportunities. Rather than feeling guilty for feeling unenthusiastic about an activity that was guaranteed to induce irritability, Lisa could have used this as a chance to have a discussion about 1) choosing an activity that makes sense given the environmental limitations, 2) being considerate of other people's preferences, and 3) working as a team to find a mutually enjoyable activity. While there are many occasions on which parents are expected to set aside their preferences for the sake of their children's enjoyment, parents need to be aware of their limitations so they don't contribute to an unpleasant situation unnecessarily.

Take Responsibility

As mentioned during the initial portion of this chapter, parents have considerable control over the trajectory of their child's behavior, particularly when they take the time to use preventative parenting to avoid misbehavior and set the stage for success. When parents are evaluating a given situation in which their child has misbehaved, parents should first examine the decisions they've made and consider whether the misbehavior could have been avoided.

Was the misbehavior the direct result of poor planning or unrealistic expectations? Did the child start off her day with the appropriate tools to succeed (sleep and adequate nutrition)? Was the child told what to expect? Did the child have the skills and motivation to meet these expectations? If so, and the child still engaged in misbehavior, were the consequences reasonable and adhered to?

Although parents need to look to themselves first when analyzing the factors that contributed to their child's misbehavior, they also need to take responsibility for their role in their child's behavioral successes. Well-developed social skills, adequate coping strategies, good sleeping and eating routines, and a developing ability to self-monitor are all skills that are introduced and fostered by parents. Sometimes our self-evaluation is too harsh, as we tend to focus on our missteps rather than our triumphs.

Key Points Discussed in Chapter 3

- Children need to be given advance warning in order to prepare physically and emotionally for a transition to a new activity. They also benefit from understanding the behavioral expectations and the potential consequences of misbehavior.

- Misbehavior can often be prevented by simply providing your child with an adequate amount of attention or active engagement. Attention (and praise) should be provided when your child is behaving appropriately.

- Be prepared with the appropriate materials to feed, clothe, and entertain your child. Remember, bored children = naughty children.

- Set realistic expectations based on your child's age. Be prepared, prioritize behavior that's important to you, and examine whether misbehavior is the result of a skill deficit or a performance deficit. If it's a skill deficit, be prepared to teach. If it's a performance deficit, be prepared to motivate. We'll discuss this further in later chapters.

- Parents, know your mood and tolerance level. Don't set yourself up to be frustrated with a particular activity or setting if you are already tired. This tends to trickle down to the children or may cause us to unfairly classify their behavior as misbehavior.

- Parents, give yourself a break. Give yourself a pat on the back and recognize that there is so much you're **already** doing right.

Chapter 4

Reinforcing Positive Behavior

We want our accomplishments to be appreciated. We like people to notice when we work hard. We aim to please people we like and admire. We want to feel pride in our work and our personal choices.

Every day, all day, we get feedback from our environment. The nature of this feedback sends messages to our brain such as, "Keep doing that." Or, "Stop it; that was a bad choice." Sometimes the messages are obvious, such as when we have to slam on the brakes because we are trying to change the song playing on our iPod® while driving. Other messages are more subtle, such as when we earn a smile from our boss after arriving to a meeting five minutes early. In the first scenario, we're likely to think twice about prioritizing our tunes above safety. In the second example, we absorb the fact that our supervisor is pleased by promptness.

Children receive similar feedback from their environment. They learn that whining may get them what they want. Crying when injured results in snuggles. Lying very quietly on the couch causes Dad to forget bedtime. Aggression results in time away from peers. As parents we have a responsibility to teach our child appropriate behavior. If a child is exhibiting a specific behavior (positive or negative), we've surely contributed to its reinforcement. Therefore, we need to be vigilant about attending

Behavior that is ignored completely is likely to be replaced by behavior that is reinforced.

to positive behavior, because when things are going smoothly, it's tempting simply to enjoy it rather than be mindful about reinforcing it. Conversely, we need to avoid reinforcing misbehavior, as this is often done inadvertently. In this chapter, we're going to focus on how to effectively use positive reinforcement to maximize desired behavior. Remember, positive reinforcement is defined as "adding something favorable to the environment for the purpose of increasing the strength or frequency of a behavior."

However, reinforcement can be sneaky. Behavior that we don't intend to reinforce can be encouraged quite easily. I'll give you an example:

Joey, a fourth grader, has a tendency to misbehave in math class nearly every day. He begins by making disruptive noises, and when reprimanded, he quickly progresses to talking back to the teacher, throwing objects, and using inappropriate language. Inevitably, the teacher asks him to spend the remainder of the class period sitting on the bench outside of the principal's office. Oftentimes, he joins another peer who also has a tendency to misbehave. After several days of this, the two boys become friends and greet each other enthusiastically when they see each other.

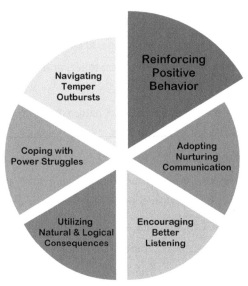

Dr. Tara Egan's Behavioral Model

Let's think this through. The misbehavior consists of disrespect toward the math teacher. The punishment is the "time-out" on the bench outside of the principal's office. However, this punishment is overshadowed by the reinforcement of making a new, like-minded friend. Ultimately, the reward of spending time with the new friend is stronger than the deterrent of a scolding by the principal or consequences administered at home. Therefore, the misbehavior is being inadvertently reinforced, increasing the likelihood that the misbehavior will reoccur.

Basic Types of Reinforcement

Physical

This can include hugs, squeezes, hair stroking, hand holding, high-fives, back patting, being picked up (if they're very young), and cheek stroking. This can also include physical representations that do not involve actually touching the child, such as winks, thumbs-up, smiles, air kisses, silly faces, etc.

Verbal

Verbal praise is reinforcement that is given through the use of affirming words. This is the most common type of reinforcement and, if used correctly, can be a very powerful motivator. Here are some tips for effective verbal reinforcement:

1. Verbal praise should be individualized. As often as possible, provide verbal praise to one child at a time, and use their name when you're addressing them.

2. Verbal praise should be given within close proximity, not called across a room or up the stairs. This allows you to make eye contact and incorporate physical touch, such as a hug, a shoulder squeeze, or a high-five.

3. Praise should be specific, highlighting the positive behavior in detail.

Riley is in her room, getting dressed for a playdate. Her mother walks by and notices that she's reaching for a T-shirt. Mom reminds her that it's supposed to be particularly cold today, so she'd like Riley to wear a sweater. Five minutes later, Riley exits her room wearing a sweater, some cute leggings, and her favorite boots.

Mom: Riley, you look great! That's a perfect outfit for today.

Riley: Really?

Mom: Yes! Turn around so I can see the back. (She takes Riley's hand and rotates her around.) I love it. You're going to be nice and warm. Thank you for listening to my suggestion to wear a sweater. You look so nice, and you're going to be able to play outside for as long as you want without getting cold. (She playfully tugs on Riley's collar, looks her in the eye, and winks.)

Privileges

Privileges, or permission to engage in an appealing activity that is not always permitted, can be a powerful motivator. For it to be effective, however, one needs to make sure the privilege is coveted by the child (giving her permission to invite her cousin over for a sleepover when she doesn't typically enjoy spending time with her cousin is not really a privilege). Examples of privileges include:

- Staying up past bedtime on the weekend

- Inviting a friend over

- Extra time with a fun activity, such as using the computer

- Going on an outing, such as to a favorite park or restaurant

- Getting to choose a family activity, such as the movie or game for family night
- Getting a "chore pass"

Time

For most children, spending time with a parent is greatly desired, particularly if it's time that is uninterrupted by work demands or another sibling. Allow the child to choose the activity, resolve to present yourself as cheerful and attentive (I realize that playing toy soldiers may not be the most stimulating activity), and inform the child as to the amount of time you're able to dedicate to them (no child wants to be given the impression that you have all afternoon to spend with him when in reality you only have one hour).

Tangible Rewards

Tangible rewards, or rewards involving a physical object, can be as simple or as complicated as you make them. Some parents use them to reinforce behavior

> Bribery can be a problem if it's used as a strategy to maintain daily behavioral standards.

and invest a considerable amount of time and money into the process. However, unless you've set a precedent that's intensive in time and/or money, this is almost never necessary. A tangible reward may consist of items such as:

- Stickers
- A favorite snack
- A home-made award
- A toy
- A book
- A game

Wait, What's the Difference between Tangible Reinforcement and Bribery?

Bribery is premeditated. The child is told that if he or she behaves in a particular way, a tangible reward will follow. The reward is *entirely* dependent **upon the child displaying that specific, *predetermined* behavior.** This tangible reward, or incentive, is intended to motivate the child to behave in the desired manner. In effect, the parent makes the statement, "If you do _____, then I'll buy or give you _____."

Examples:

If you drive safely for a year after you get your license, I'll help you pay for a new car.

If you get an A on your report card, I'll buy you a video game.

If you behave in the grocery store, I'll let you pick out a piece of candy in the checkout line.

In contrast, tangible reinforcement simply means that you use a tangible item to reinforce behavior. This type of reinforcement is usually administered intermittently in an attempt to send the message "Keep doing this." The behavior reinforced is not predetermined.

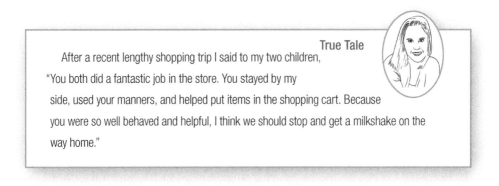

True Tale

After a recent lengthy shopping trip I said to my two children, "You both did a fantastic job in the store. You stayed by my side, used your manners, and helped put items in the shopping cart. Because you were so well behaved and helpful, I think we should stop and get a milkshake on the way home."

In this example, I provided verbal praise and a tangible reward. But because I didn't dangle the prospect of a milkshake in front of them before the shopping trip, it didn't meet the definition of bribery.

Bribery is most appropriate when trying to motivate your child to attempt a particular activity that is low incidence/high anxiety (such as undergoing a dental procedure). It should be noted that relying on bribery can interfere with the development of intrinsic motivation, which we will discuss later in this chapter.

How to Choose the Type of Reinforcement

Everyone has preferred modes of communication. More specifically, everyone has a personalized method of "hearing" information. When you're trying to convey a positive message to someone, they are most likely to "hear" you (or receive that message) if you deliver it in the way they find most understandable and rewarding.

Dr. Gary Chapman, author of the phenomenon known as *The 5 Love Languages* (2010), discusses this very topic in detail. Although he originally applied it to married couples, he indicates that people are most responsive to positive messages conveyed in their preferred style. Specifically, he indicates that there are five "love languages." Although individuals may "hear" love when two or three types of "love languages" are conveyed (and conversely, will not "hear" the other types at all), most people have a clear preference as to how they wish others would communicate positive messages toward them. Because I'm using Dr. Chapman's approach to illustrate a point rather than tout it specifically, I'll simply note his five "love languages" in a peripheral way:

1. **Words of Affirmation:** These include unsolicited compliments, being told reasons why you are loved and appreciated.

2. **Quality Time:** Love is conveyed when another person dedicates time doing something that you enjoy, especially when it's apparent that they are participating as a gesture of love toward you. Of course, the time dedicated must not simply consist of the person's presence; it should include active engagement such as eye contact, undivided attention, and an appropriate emotional response.

3. **Receiving Gifts:** This means receiving tangible items such thoughtful gifts or trinkets.

4. **Acts of Service:** These include completing unpleasant obligations for you, like household chores or attending an unappealing social function.

5. **Physical Touch:** Love is conveyed through physical affection, such as hugs, kisses, massage, etc.

Parents need to try and figure out which of the love languages will be best received by their child. In turn, they need to explore their own preferences and compare and contrast them with their child's preferences. While it may be relatively effortless to communicate with your child when your love languages are similar, parents will have to be more conscious about speaking a language that doesn't come naturally. For example, your love language may be "words of affirmation," so in an attempt to convey love to your child, you leave her little notes on her bed with encouraging statements like, "You'll do great on your history exam today! You studied so hard!" However, if her love language differs from yours, e.g., "acts of service," your love may actually be better conveyed when you drive her willingly to a friend's house or help her clean her room. Parents must make a conscious effort to determine their child's love language or else they are at risk of communicating in a manner that is less than ideal for their child.

Note that of these five "love languages," four of them have clear parallels to the types of reinforcements described earlier in this chapter. This is relevant information when it comes time to decide how to best reinforce your child. After all, you want them to *hear* and *feel* this reinforcement, in hopes that they will be encouraged to repeat a desired behavior. For example, I regularly work with a little boy named Hayden, age seven. He struggles to identify his emotions, follow through with directions, and monitor his impulse control. He greatly benefits from being reinforced with physical touch, and I'd go so far as to say that he will not "hear" me at all if physical touch isn't utilized.

Me: Hayden, I need to tell you something. Come here.

Hayden: What? (He approaches willingly and stands in front of me.)

Me (crouching down, making eye contact, grasping his shoulders gently, and sliding my hands down his arms): I'm so proud of you for making the choice to walk away when Ben called you an idiot.

Hayden: Yeah.

Me: I need to tell you three things that I like about what you did. (I take his hand, spread his fingers, and touch the pad of each finger as I speak.) First, I like that you didn't yell at him. Second, I like that you walked away. And third, I like that you found someone else to play with on your own.

Hayden: (grins)

Me: So thank you for making such a good choice today. I hope you're proud of yourself, because I certainly am.

Hayden: (still grinning)

Me (giving his hand one last squeeze): Now, go play. It looks like those boys want to play soccer.

The reinforcement would not have been as meaningful to Hayden had physical touch not been used. I had to modify my use of reinforcement to account for how he "hears" positive messages.

Tips for Using Reinforcement Effectively

1. *"Catch" your child behaving; attend to the positive behavior.*

As has been said elsewhere in this book, attention is inherently reinforcing, regardless of whether the attention offered is positive (e.g., in the form of praise) or negative (e.g., yelling). If misbehavior is attended to, then that's the behavior we're more likely to see in the future.

Jacob and Rebecca are playing nicely in the backyard while Mom is working in the garden. Every so often, Mom peeks around the corner of the house, sees them playing appropriately, and returns to her work. She's relieved that they are cooperating enough for her to get some work done. After about 30 minutes, she hears them arguing and goes to investigate. She finds Jacob shoving dirt down the back of Rebecca's shirt while she screeches at him and tries to throw dirt in his face. Mom breaks up their argument, provides sympathy as Rebecca plaintively describes Jacob's wrongdoing, and instructs them to clean up the dirt on the patio. She ends up helping them sweep up the dirt and tells them that she wants to work on the garden for another hour. Within ten minutes, they're arguing again. She sighs and gives up on today's project.

First of all, let's acknowledge a scenario like this is going to happen, regardless of the mindfulness of your parenting. It's inevitable that children who are left to their own devices are going to struggle with self-control at some point. However, considering the fact that attention is inherently reinforcing, it may have been more helpful if Mom had attended to the appropriate behavior (playing nicely), rather than only making her presence known when the children were misbehaving.

Let's try this again.

Jacob and Rebecca are playing nicely in the backyard while Mom is working in the garden. Every so often, Mom peeks around the corner of the house, and, if she finds them playing appropriately, she makes it a point to approach them and give them some positive feedback about their good behavior.

Mom: Hi, you two. I just finished trimming the rose bushes and next I'm going to do some weeding. I appreciate your playing together so nicely. Tell me about what you're doing.

Rebecca: We're building a little town in the dirt.

Jacob: Yeah, we have tunnels, and these little plastic men are the town leaders.

Mom: That's pretty cool (she reaches down and points to something). What's that?

Jacob: That's the school. Soon there's going to be a flood (he gestures to a large cup of water that he's obviously going to use to flood the town).

Mom: I see. Well, I'm going to want to see the flooded town, so come get me when you do it. In the meantime, I'm going to work on the weeding. Give me at least 15 minutes before you come get me, okay?

Rebecca: Okay. We're going to build a moat!

Mom: Awesome. I love that idea. You guys are using some great teamwork.

Twenty minutes later, Rebecca comes to get her mother to see their flooded town. Mom thanks her for remembering to include her, finishes the section she's weeding, and follows Rebecca back to the pile of dirt they're playing in. Jacob excitedly tells her about the flood, the moat, and their plan to rebuild the town. Mom marvels at their imagination, praises them for working together, and returns to her work. This continues for another hour, with Mom checking in twice more. Each time Mom checks in on the children, she makes sure they are doing something positive before she gives them extensive attention, as she wants her attention to reward the positive behavior.

2. Regardless of the type of reinforcement used, administer it with sincerity.

In order for reinforcement to be effective, it needs to be administered in a sincere, thoughtful way. For example, if tangible rewards are to be used, the item gifted should demonstrate that the parent used thought when choosing the item, even if it's something without monetary value. If it's praise, be specific and make eye contact. If it's time spent with a parent, make it unrushed and child-driven.

Aiden, age five, is at soccer practice. Prior to today, he's struggled to listen and follow directions and try his best. Today, he is able to kick the ball impressively far at the beginning of practice. His coach is enthusiastic in his praise, and Aiden excitedly calls to his dad (who is standing on the sidelines with another father, talking), "Look, Dad! I kicked the ball really far!" Dad responds by calling back, "Good job!" and immediately returns to his conversation. Aiden feels deflated, as he knows that his father hasn't even heard what he's said, let alone seen his accomplishment.

Kids realize when you're being insincere.

Use Secondary Praise. Children Love It, and It Works

Secondary praise, or overheard verbal praise, is an easy way to convey pride in your child's good choices. Children are accustomed to verbal praise being administered directly, from adult to child. Secondary praise, in contrast, is when a parent praises a child to another person and the child can overhear it.

In this scenario, Mom is on the telephone with Grandma. Her son, Reese, age five, is playing with his toys in a nearby room.

Mom: Mom, you should have seen your grandson yesterday. I was so proud of him. The entire family was at a restaurant, and we had to wait a long time for our food. I know Reese was really hungry, but he was able to stay in his seat the entire time. When our food finally came, he used his manners, wiped off the table with his napkin, and reminded me not to leave our leftovers on the table as we were leaving. He's getting to be such a big boy, and I love going places with him when he's so well behaved.

Just think: If you overheard your boss speaking about you in glowing terms, how would you feel? I'd hazard a guess and say fantastic.

Intrinsic vs. Extrinsic Motivation

Motivation, or the general desire to do something, comes in two forms. *Extrinsic motivation* is when the desire to behave in a specific way is elicited by external forces, or stimuli that are outside of the person. Some common extrinsic motivators are:

Money	Verbal praise	Physical affection	A good report card
Candy	Smiles	Prizes/Awards	A raise or promotion
Stickers	High-fives	Privileges	Attention

The types of reinforcement discussed in this chapter thus far have all been extrinsic motivators.

In contrast, *intrinsic motivation* is when a desire to behave in a specific way is elicited by an internal reward, such as pride, a sense of self-worth, heightened self-esteem, or a sense of accomplishment. Intrinsic rewards are non-tangible and directly related to the mindset of the individual. In order to embrace a behavior intrinsically, the individual has to have an inherent belief in the value of the behavior.

Here are some examples of behaviors that are the result of intrinsic motivation:

- High achievement in school
- Treating others with respect and kindness
- Contributing meaningfully to a charity or worthy cause
- Volunteering your time

So, why have we focused so much on extrinsic motivators in this chapter if intrinsic motivation is where it's at?

Well, for a couple of reasons:

1. *Sometimes we're expected to do things that we don't enjoy.*

For example, we may get up and go to a ho-hum job every day because of the paycheck, an extrinsic motivator. We may remember to have our parents sign our agenda book each day because it will earn us a free ice cream cone from the school cafeteria. We may complete chores on Saturday morning because we know Dad will watch a movie with us on Saturday evening if everything around the house is done. Sometimes we do things simply because we have to, and an extrinsic motivator makes it more bearable.

> Intrinsic motivators are believed to be more inherently reinforcing than extrinsic motivators.

2. *Extrinsic rewards can lead to intrinsic satisfaction.*

Unless there is an external motivator, we may never try something new or anxiety-provoking. And if we don't ever try it, there is certainly no chance of it ever evolving into a source of intrinsic motivation. For example, think of the overweight man whose wife promises to allot him ten dollars toward season tickets to his favorite football team every time he goes to the gym and takes a fitness class. After weeks of attending fitness classes only to make progress toward that extrinsic reward of season tickets, he begins to notice that he's losing weight, has increased energy, and feels more handsome. Soon, he's thinking less about the season tickets and more about how exercise makes him feel. A behavior that was initially extrinsically motivated has now transformed into an intrinsically motivated behavior. As a result, he's much more likely to continue to exercise after the football season is over.

3. The ability to be intrinsically motivated is a developmental milestone.

Small children don't have the critical thinking skills or the life experience to understand that some behavior should be displayed just because it's the right thing to do and it feels good. They need some concrete feedback from the environment that says, "Keep doing this." For example, young children initially learn to follow the rules because it results in verbal praise, physical touch, and tangible rewards. After a while, they begin to realize that rules exist for a reason—they provide consistency and structure and help people maintain self-control. Eventually, most children follow society's rules because they're intrinsically motivated to do so, not because they are simply avoiding a punishment should they get caught. As children age, their capacity to develop intrinsic motivation for select behavior is enhanced.

Final Thoughts

Now that we've discussed how to reinforce positive behavior when it's observed, we need to take a moment and recall that positive behavior cannot be displayed if the child does not know how to demonstrate it (if they have a skill deficit). If you witness a positive behavior, reinforce it. If you observe misbehavior, make sure you *do not* inadvertently reinforce it. Take the time to teach and practice the preferred behavior.

Good behavior needs to be taught.
Good behavior has to be role-modeled.
Good behavior needs to be reinforced.
Often.

Key Points Discussed in Chapter 4

- Feedback we get from our environment can reinforce or punish our behavior. If behavior is reinforced, it's more likely to be repeated.

- Positive reinforcement is defined as "adding something favorable to the environment for the purpose of increasing the strength or frequency of a behavior." However, it's very easy to reinforce misbehavior inadvertently.

- There are several basic types of reinforcement: physical, verbal, privileges, time, and tangible rewards.

- The primary difference between tangible rewards and bribery is that bribery is premeditated. A bribe is promised prior to the positive behavior being displayed. In contrast, a tangible reward is simply used to send a message after the positive behavior is demonstrated to "keep doing that."

- Bribery is most appropriate when trying to motivate your child to attempt a particular activity that is low incidence/high anxiety.

- Gary Chapman identifies five love languages in which positive messages can be conveyed: words of affirmation, quality time, receiving gifts, acts of service, and physical touch. Your child will be most responsive to positive reinforcement that is conveyed via his or her primary love language.

- Two tips to use reinforcement effectively are to 1) "catch" your child behaving and attend to positive behavior and 2) administer reinforcement with sincerity.

- Extrinsic motivation is when the desire to behave in a specific way is elicited by external forces—stimuli that are outside of the person. In contrast, intrinsic motivation is when a desire to behave in a specific way is elicited by an internal reward, such as pride or enhanced self-esteem. Intrinsic motivators are believed to be more inherently reinforcing.

Chapter 5

Adopting a Nurturing Communication Style and Encouraging Better Listening

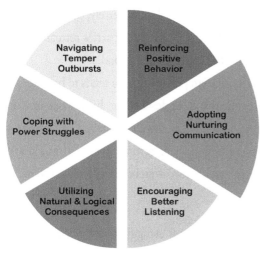

Dr. Tara Egan's Behavioral Model

So much of my work with parents consists of reframing their understanding of effective communication between a parent and a child. We may adopt a specific way of interacting with our children that, if inadequate, can compound problems and impact the overall quality of the relationship. However, if our communication style is respectful and nurturing, it can be used as a proactive strategy to encourage positive behavior and address problem behavior in a productive and healthy way. The communication style described in this chapter—if adopted with mindfulness and consistency—is a relatively simple intervention that will benefit your parent-child relationship immeasurably.

Parenting Styles

Developmental psychologists have long investigated the relationship between parent-child communication and the overall happiness, adjustment, and social competence of children. Diana Baumrind's (1967) pivotal research identified four primary parenting styles.

Authoritarian

According to Baumrind (1967), authoritarian parents establish rules characterized by inflexibility and dominance. Opposition is met with punishment and reinforcement is minimal or absent. Children often don't understand the reasoning behind the rules. Behavioral expectations are high, although there is little responsiveness to a child's emotions.

In my experience, parents who demonstrate an authoritarian parenting style often produce children who are either relatively unassertive and struggle with low self-esteem *or* are oppositional, resentful, and eager to rebel. Oftentimes, the relationship between the parents and child is fraught with power struggles, with the parent dominating until the child's behavior becomes extreme and "out of control." Conversely, the relationship may become so fraught with arguments and turmoil that both parties retreat to their separate corners feeling defeated, disconnected, and misunderstood.

The language and tone used by an authoritarian parenting style tends to be dour and negative. These parents often sound impatient and condescending. Even when making statements with neutral wording, they can present as critical or harsh. They appear to struggle to enjoy their children, and seem to anticipate getting embroiled in a power struggle long before one is present. These parents can often be classified as "yellers."

Permissive

According to Baumrind (1967), permissive parents struggle to establish standards for good behavior. They have low expectations for their child's ability to self-regulate and demonstrate maturity, and they are oftentimes so consumed with protecting their child's emotional state that they refrain from setting healthy boundaries. They avoid making demands in a quest to avoid power struggles or confrontation.

In my experience, parents who demonstrate a permissive parenting style struggle to establish themselves as an authority figure for their child. These are the parents who "bend the rules" and struggle to remain consistent with their behavioral strategies and planned consequences. Their children are more likely to whine or act bossy, crave structure, and be overemotional. These parents struggle with feelings of guilt when their child isn't successful, and oftentimes they make excuses for their child's behavior rather than holding the child accountable. These are the parents who are most likely to ask for help, particularly if they are the primary caretaker of the children.

The language and tone used by a permissive parent tend to be tentative, questioning, or pleading. These parents often placate, bribe, and use praise excessively and indiscriminately. When attempting to discipline, these parents offer too much explanation and pepper their words with assurances of love. If these parents are driven to raise their voice or otherwise express frustration, their words often have an emotional undertone.

Uninvolved

According to Baumrind (1967), uninvolved parents remain detached from the more subtle aspects of parenting, such as teaching prosocial behaviors and remaining responsive to emotional cues.

In my experience, uninvolved parents tend to remain in "denial" of their child's misbehaviors and adopt an approach that is nonconfrontational. Unlike permissive parents, their nonconfrontational attitude stems from a failure to get invested, rather than from a fear of bruising their child's emotions. They tend to appease in an uninterested way and leave the tough parenting moments to the co-parent, an outside resource, or the school professionals. In a household, an uninvolved parent is often counterbalanced by a permissive parent.

The language and tone of uninvolved parents is most characterized by mild directives with little follow-through, or impatience followed by detachment.

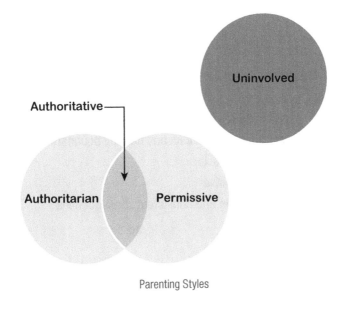

Parenting Styles

Authoritative

The fourth parenting style described by Baumrind (1967) is authoritative, and it is generally perceived to be the most beneficial to children's overall adjustment. According to Baumrind (1967), authoritative parents are able to balance the need for rules and structure with an ability to respond to their child's emotional needs. They permit children to ask questions and account for their opinions, but ultimately they feel comfortable asserting themselves as the adult charged with providing boundaries and guidance. Misbehavior is met with clear consequences and forgiveness.

In my experience, authoritative parents understand the role of reinforcing positive behavior and discouraging misbehavior through the use of fair and reasonable consequences. These parents are firm but not overly punitive. They protect their child's feelings but understand that they have a responsibility to expose their child to both the joyful and the sorrowful moments of life. These parents hold their children accountable for their choices. They leave room for a suitable expression of emotion, yet they expect an age-appropriate level of maturity, self-control, and independence. They provide choices when appropriate but understand that offering options is not always feasible.

The language and tone exhibited by an authoritative parent are characterized by clarity, a positive, upbeat tone, mild humor, and overt confidence in their child's ability to adhere to expectations. These parents adopt what I refer to as a "nurturing communication style."

Authoritative parenting has several positive characteristics, including:
- Balancing the need for rules with a responsiveness to emotion
- Balancing the child's need to ask questions and make choices with the need to set high expectations and healthy boundaries
- Reinforcing positive behavior
- Being firm, but not punitive
- Administering clear, fair, and consistent consequences

Nurturing Communication

What Is It?

The concept I refer to as "nurturing communication" is a specific style of communication between family members—more specifically, between a parent and a child. It's intended to be warm, respectful, and supportive, yet convey high behavioral expectations. Nurturing communication is sensitive to the emotional needs of the child, yet it isn't characterized by the indulgence or tentativeness of the permissive parent or the excessive firmness and inflexibility of the authoritarian parent. It gives the impression that you're collaborating with your child, rather than appearing deferential or commanding. Basically, you're exhibiting an appealing communication style that results in your child's feeling invested in your expectations, rather than feeling cajoled or bullied.

Components of Nurturing Language

Nurturing communication is comprised of three characteristics, all of which are designed to demonstrate engagement, respect, and healthy expectations and boundaries.

Language

The language, or the actual words used, is extremely important when adopting a nurturing communication style with a child. The language used is always respectful and easily understood. Empathy, or demonstrating an understanding of the child's feelings, is essential. The parent is firm and consistent with expectations, favors encouraging statements, and uses verbal praise in a genuine, selective manner. Their words demonstrate that they value their child. These parents tend to ask age-appropriate questions and explain their decisions in a simple, relatable way. They account for a child's feelings and need for structure by providing advance notice and describing consequences ahead of time. The language of a parent using nurturing communication is not one characterized by disrespect and shame.

Tone

The tone, or attitude, conveyed by a parent's words is the second aspect of a nurturing communication style. The tone portrayed is one of warmth, encouragement, and gentle humor. It's upbeat and illustrates that a parent has confidence in their parenting choices and an inherent belief in the child's ability to succeed. The tone of a parent using nurturing communication is not characterized by negativity or impatience.

Physical Touch

Physical touch, the third aspect of the nurturing communication style, consists of any visual representation of a thought or feeling. For example, pride in your child may be expressed by a huge grin, a thumbs-up, or an exuberant hug. Sympathy may be expressed by hand-holding, a lengthy hug, or stroking a back. Disappointment may be revealed by a facial expression or a brief reduction in eye contact. How physical touch is used can greatly enhance the messages sent from parent to child. Physical touch by a parent using nurturing communication is not characterized by deliberate roughness.

Adopting a Nurturing Communication Style

It is possible for all parents and families to adopt a nurturing communication style with patience and practice. Take some time to examine your current method of communication and slowly begin to substitute its most ineffective aspects with words, tone, and touch that are compatible with the nurturing communication style. The positive response you receive from your child is likely to reinforce your change in communication style, making it easier to continue and more rewarding. Many parents feel that this component of the behavioral model results in the most prominent change in their family life, as it encourages the climate in the home to become warmer, more supportive, and more collaborative. This, in turn, prevents tension that can later progress into temper outbursts and power struggles. Let's consider some examples.

Mom comes home from work and finds her 10-year-old daughter curled on the couch, gazing at the TV. Her daughter appears fatigued and possibly irritable.

Mom: Hey sweetie! How was your day? I thought of you today when I was eating my pizza at lunch. It had pepperoni on it, and I wished you were there to eat it with me.

(Message sent: warmth, affection, missing her daughter throughout the day. Gives a specific detail to imply sincerity.)

Evelyn (gaze remains directed toward television): Hey.

Mom (approaches Evelyn, sits next to her on the couch, and squeezes her foot briefly): How are you? You seem a little tired.

(Message: empathy, attentiveness, but no pressure. Accompanies her message with physical touch.)

Evelyn (shrugs): I'm okay. Just watching this show.

Mom: Okay. (She sits with her for two or three minutes, waiting to see if Evelyn wants to give any more details about her day, especially since she seems subdued.) Well, watch another 15 minutes and then come into the kitchen and keep me company while I make dinner. I'll make the salad and you set the table.

(Note the advance warning of a behavioral expectation. The expectation was stated simply, not asked or presented as an option.)

Evelyn (groans and stretches sleepily): Do I have to?

Mom: Yes, because I hate having to eat my food without any plates or forks. If you don't set the table, we're all going to have to act like animals in a barn and eat with our paws. (Mom mimics eating messily, like a barn animal.)

Evelyn (laughs): Gross, Mom. Can we have soup with it?

Mom (rising off the couch): If we have some. I'll go check and let you know when you come to help. I'll see you in a few minutes. Do you care what kind of soup?

(Notice she says "when you help," not "if." The implication is that she has confidence that her daughter will comply with her directive. She's also promoting a "team" atmosphere by pointing out that they will both be doing tasks to prepare for dinner. She also asks Evelyn's opinion.)

Evelyn: Maybe tomato?

Mom: Mmm. Sounds good.

(10 minutes later)

Mom: Evelyn, my helpful girl (she stands at the doorway, smiling)…come and help me. I'm ready for you in the kitchen. I'm hoping that you get so distracted by our conversation that I can just sit around while you do all the work. (Mom grins and winks.)

Evelyn (giggles): No, Mom, you have to help too! You're making the salad, remember?

Mom (grinning): What? I have no memory of saying that. I said I was going to help by eating all the carrots you cut up. And I'll save all the dishes for you, because I love you and I'm sweet like that.

Evelyn (rising off the couch and following her mother into the kitchen): Funny, Mom. A deal's a deal.

Mom: Alright. (She grins and gently tugs a lock of her daughter's hair as she walks by.)

In the above scenario, Mom set the tone of the conversation by showing attentiveness, affection, and a positive demeanor. She gives an advance warning of a behavioral expectation, uses age-appropriate humor to address Evelyn's initial reluctance to comply, and never placates, pleads, or wavers in her expectation. She recognizes that there is no need to raise her voice or give a command.

Landon, a second grade student, arrives home from school, where his father is waiting. Their routine is to have a snack and then start homework. After Landon eats, his father urges him to start his homework.

Dad: Did you have a good snack?

Landon: Yeah. These crackers are good.

Dad: What's the homework situation tonight? Math? Spelling?

Landon: Both. The math is hard.

Dad: Luckily I passed math in second grade and I'm here to help if you need me.

(Dad smiles and makes eye contact.)

Dad: Here you go, buddy. (He hands Landon a pencil, sending a clear message that he needs to get started.)

(Landon gets out his math assignment and writes his name on the top. He starts working. His dad stays nearby, sorting through the mail. Just by lingering nearby, he's sending a message that he's interested and attentive, although he's giving Landon the space to work independently.)

Landon: Dad, I can't do this! (Landon speaks in a whiny tone.)

Dad (cheerfully): No whining, Landon. Ask me like a big boy and I'm happy to help.

Landon (in a normal voice): Dad, can you help me?

Dad: Sure. Which math problem are you doing?

Landon: This one here.

Dad: Ahhh, you added instead of subtracted. See the subtraction sign?

Landon: Yes, okay.

Dad: I think you've got this. Just take a look at the sign of each problem. I'll check it over when you're done. Take your time.

(Landon works quietly for several minutes. He flips his page over, sees several more problems, and gets frustrated.)

Landon: Arggh! I'm not doing this! It's taking forever!

Dad: Let's see . . . You've got six more problems to do. You can finish them up or take a five-minute break and then finish them. If you're feeling really frustrated, take a break. It's okay to take a break if it helps you to come back and do good work.

(Dad sets the behavioral expectation that the homework will be finished, but acknowledges Landon's emotional state and gives a healthy suggestion to cope with it.)

Landon: I'm going to watch TV.

Dad: No, that's not a good decision. You might get caught up in a television show and then your math is going to be even less fun. You can work on your spelling homework or go walk the dog if you'd like.

(The "no" is firmly stated and a brief, reasonable expectation is given. An alternate behavior is suggested, and a choice is given.)

Landon: I want to watch TV!

Dad: Not right now, Landon. Maybe when all your homework is done. If you're too upset to make a good decision about this now, go take a break in your room until you're ready to work on your homework again.

(This is basically saying, "You'll be asked to go to time-out if you keep fussing about this." Dad avoids a power struggle by not engaging in extensive conversation about Landon's entertainment option during his "break" from math homework. P.S. Also, this statement wouldn't be made if there were a television in Landon's room.)

Landon (huffy sigh): Okay, I'll walk the dog.

Dad: Okay. I'll be here when you get back, and I can help if you need it.

Nurturing communication, to be effective, has to become part of the overall culture within your home. It must be role-modeled by all the adults within the home, both toward the children and one another. A clear message needs to be sent to the children that "this is how we communicate with each other in this home," with the intent that the children will adopt this same communication style in response. Nurturing communication is most powerful if it's used consistently and sincerely, not simply on occasion or only when you'd like your child to comply with a specific direction.

Nurturing communication is designed to eliminate the need to yell, bribe, or give ultimatums, all of which are unproductive and compromise dignity. It's a style of communication that is warm, clear, and engaging. If cultivated, it will enhance the relationship between family members, resulting in fewer conflicts and greater closeness.

As we discuss more in-depth in Chapter 9, nurturing communication is essential to establishing respect within the home.

Encouraging Better Listening

As noted above, nurturing communication is a proactive strategy used to encourage positive behavior. One of the consequences of transitioning from an ineffective style of

Dr. Tara Egan's Behavioral Model

communicating to a nurturing communication style is the immediate improvement in listening behavior. "They just don't listen" is one of the most common complaints I hear upon meeting a family. These frustrated parents report that their days are filled with giving directives that aren't attended to or adhered to, and they feel like they have to get increasingly loud and angry before their voice will permeate through their child's haze of self-absorption. This section will discuss how to incorporate our newfound knowledge about nurturing communication with best practices in encouraging better listening. As a result, you will have the tools necessary to raise children who comply with directions *and* feel valued and supported.

Tips to Improve Your Child's Listening

Although there's no way to ensure that your child will listen to (and follow!) your directions, there are ways to maximize its likelihood.

1. *Make sure that your child has the ability to follow your directions.*

Remember back in Chapter 3 when we talked about a "skill deficit" vs. a "performance deficit"?

When a child doesn't listen, most of the time it's related to a performance deficit. The child is unmotivated to stop what he or she is doing, attend to the direction, and carry it out. However, before you lose your temper, ask yourself if your child *can* do what you're asking without extraordinary effort. In order to assess this, recall the principles described in Chapter 2 in which we discussed the Whole Child. Are you asking him to navigate a tricky social situation for which he's not developmentally prepared? Are you asking her to follow multistep directions, and she's getting confused and frustrated because she's hungry or tired? Have you considered his sensory needs, such as whether the noisy environment is interfering with his ability to attend to and understand the directions? You may be able to address the environmental variables that are impacting your child's ability to listen and consequently enhance his or her compliance.

> A skill deficit is when a child cannot display the behavior. They don't know how.
> A performance deficit is when a child can display the behavior but does not or will not.

Once you've ruled out the possibility of their failure to listen resulting from a skill deficit, it's necessary to take care that you're conveying your directives in the most clear, child-friendly manner possible.

True Tale

I, personally, am guilty of calling directions up the stairwell to a child whom I cannot see. The scenario goes something like this:

Me: I need you guys to get dressed so you can come downstairs and eat breakfast!

Them: (uninterrupted sounds of playing)

Me: Guys! Do you hear me?

One to the other: Shhh! I think Mom just said something!

(continued)

> *Me: Guys!*
>
> *Them: What?*
>
> *Me: I need you two to get dressed so you can come down and eat breakfast!*
>
> *Them: Okay! (They resume playing, almost as if I hadn't spoken.)*
>
> *Me (Ten minutes later): Hey, you two!*
>
> *Them: What?*
>
> *Me: Are you dressed? I asked you to get dressed ten minutes ago!*
>
> *Them: Oh! Okay, we're getting dressed now!*
>
> And this conversation is 70 percent likely to be repeated ten minutes later.
>
> Now, when this same conversation takes place with me standing six feet away, making eye contact, and referring to each child by name, there is a different response. It may go something like this:
>
> *Me: Savannah, can you come here, please? Declan, you too.*
>
> *Savannah: What?*
>
> *Declan: What, Mom?*
>
> *Me: Come here, please. To the bottom of the stairs.*
>
> *(They comply. I make eye contact with Savannah first.)*
>
> *Me: Savannah, I'd like you to get dressed so you can come down and eat breakfast.*
>
> *Savannah: Okay.*
>
> *Me: It should only take you about five minutes, so I'm going to start making your breakfast now.*
>
> *Savannah: Okay.*
>
> *Me: Thanks, sweetie. I'll see you in a few minutes. Declan (eye contact transfers to him), I'm going to need you to get dressed too. You must be getting hungry.*
>
> *Declan: Yeah, I'm hungry. Can I have a bagel, please?*
>
> *Me: Sure. I'll make it while you get dressed. I'll see you in five minutes.*

2. *Use proximity. Refer to the child by name. Make eye contact.*

As the examples above illustrate, children will have an increased sense of urgency to follow directions if they interpret your instructions to be specific and personalized.

3. *Prioritize your directions and keep them simple.*

There are dozens, if not hundreds, of behaviors that you'd like your child to exhibit each day. And as parents, we feel a sense of responsibility to guide, direct, and manage these behaviors. If you listen closely, you'll notice that much of the conversation you have with your child is embedded with directions.

Just think of a simple daily routine, such as a child getting home from school, getting a snack, and starting his homework. Your side of the conversation may go something like this:

> *Josh, where's your backpack? We have to make sure I remember to sign your agenda book, because Mrs. Harris takes points off each week if a parent doesn't sign. Go ahead, <u>get it out</u> and <u>set it on the table</u>. What do you want for snack? I have crackers and peanut butter or apples and cheese. Can you <u>grab the cheese</u> while you're over by the fridge? Did you see that I bought that juice you like? You can have some of it; just <u>get a clean cup</u> out of the dishwasher. So, <u>tell me</u> what happened at school today. Did Mrs. Harris return your math test? Make sure you <u>show it to me</u> if you have it with you. Ugh, <u>please don't</u> kick off your shoes in the middle of the kitchen. <u>Put your shoes by the door</u> so no one trips on them. And the dog is begging for some attention; he's been waiting for you. <u>Can you walk him</u> after you finish your snack? Oh, you have soccer practice later. I washed your soccer jersey but you'll have to <u>get it out</u> of the dryer. Let's <u>get started</u> on your homework; your agenda book says you have math, spelling, and reading. Let's start with the math—<u>can you find a pencil</u> with an eraser?*

From Mom's perspective, she's just making conversation—finding out about her son's day and getting his materials (his agenda book, his snack, his soccer uniform) organized. But in reality, that brief paragraph contains a dozen directions—and all are fired at Josh within the span of a few minutes. When so much of our interactions with our child are littered with directions, children start to ignore those they feel are nonessential. They do this as a coping strategy, as focusing on each direction would make them feel overwhelmed and stressed.

Therefore, be mindful of how much of your conversation is peppered with directions. Many children are unable to follow multistep directions that appear to be on random, disparate topics. In the above example, Mom gives directions about homework materials, a snack, shoes, the dog, and the soccer jersey. These are all topics that are relatively unrelated to one another. In contrast, which directions did Mom most want Josh to follow? Possibly 1) choosing a snack and 2) getting out the materials for his homework.

To simplify things, Mom can prioritize her directions so they focus on the most important topics, and consequently, make an effort to make sure all multistep directions pertain to the same topic. See below:

> *Josh, where's your backpack? We have to make sure I remember to sign your agenda book, because Mrs. Harris takes points off each week if a parent doesn't sign. Go ahead, <u>get it out</u> and <u>set it on the table</u>. Did your teacher return your math test? I'd like to see it. Let's <u>get started</u> on your homework; your agenda book says you have math, spelling, and reading. Let's start with the math—<u>can you find a pencil</u> with an eraser?*

In this example, there were still several directions for Josh to follow, but they were all related to the topic of getting ready to do homework. In general, if Mom can see that he is getting out his materials in preparation to complete his homework, she'll feel satisfied that he is listening.

However, there are some children who, even if given directions that are relevant, can get easily overwhelmed and flustered. These children may need directions to be broken down further and possibly only given one at a time. Again, consider the Whole Child when giving directions:

> *Josh, where's your backpack? We have to make sure I remember to sign your agenda book, because Mrs. Harris takes points off each week if a parent doesn't sign. Go ahead, <u>get it out</u> and <u>set it on the table</u>.*
>
> *(Mom waits until he gets out his agenda book and sets it on the table.)*
>
> *Let's see. <u>Josh, can you take everything out of the agenda</u> book for me? I'm interested to see if your teacher returned your math test.*
>
> *(Josh rifles through and retrieves the math test.)*
>
> *Thanks! Look, you only got one question wrong! Fantastic! Let's show this to Dad later; he'll be so proud. Now, what do you have to do for homework tonight? Math, spelling, and reading. Let's get started. <u>Can you find a pencil</u> with an eraser?*

In this scenario, Mom gives one direction at a time, and offers *wait time* between each direction. When Josh complies, she acknowledges that he has complied with the direction (and offers some minor praise in the form of a thank you, etc.) before giving a new direction. She sits close by, uses his name, and makes eye contact. This keeps Josh focused, attentive, and more likely to follow the directions.

4. Tell children what TO do, not what NOT to do.

Oftentimes, we are content to simply assume that our children know what to do. After all, they know what their bedtime routine is, right? They've been doing the same thing for years! However, when they veer off course and need directions, we tend to simply chastise, rather than correct or reteach. We need to provide directions that are truly directive, not just plaintive. This is clearly compatible with a nurturing communication style, as we hope to be clear and respectful rather than negative or commanding.

What NOT to Do	What TO Do
"Peyton, don't throw your towel on the floor."	"Peyton, hang up your towel on the hook, please."
"Jake, stop that. You're making a mess."	"Jake, please get a sponge and wipe up the crumbs."
"Jenna, don't just sit there."	"Jenna, get out your science homework and take a seat at the kitchen table, please."

5. Check for comprehension.

Sometimes the best way to determine whether your child understands your directions is to simply observe them. If the child is complying, your directions are probably understood. If they're not, then it may be that the child is confused, needs clarification, or simply needs the directions repeated to help with recall.

Sometimes, checking for comprehension might just be asking the child to repeat back what you've just said:

Mom: Sarah, I need you to go upstairs and brush your teeth, comb your hair, and get your shoes.

Sarah: Okay.

Mom: So, what did I ask you to do, sweetheart?

Sarah: Brush my teeth, comb my hair, and . . .

Mom: Get your shoes.

Sarah: Right. Brush teeth, comb hair, get shoes.

Mom: Exactly. Thanks, honey.

Other times, checking for comprehension may be a bit more subtle:

Dad: Will, can you go out to the garage and bring back a socket wrench? I need it to put together this bookshelf. And can you grab the sockets too? I need several sizes. They should be in the black tool chest.

Will: Sure, Dad.

Dad: Do you know where the black tool chest is?

Will: Yeah, it's next to the cabinet with all the paint cans in it.

Dad: Right. I just need the socket wrench and the sockets that go with it. Are you familiar with what those are?

Will: Yeah, the sockets are in that little red plastic case.

Dad: Great, thank you. I really appreciate your help.

6. *Praise (if necessary, praise for each step completed correctly).*

The act of following directions is a desired behavior. Therefore, to increase its likelihood of happening in the future, children should be reinforced when they listen. As described in Chapter 4, reinforcement sends children the message to "keep doing that." There are two aspects of "listening" behavior to consider when offering praise or reinforcement:

- **Praising the specific behavior exhibited**

  This refers to praising a child directly upon his completion of a specific directive. "Thank you, Jayden, for cleaning up the toys when I asked you to. That was very helpful."

- **Praising overall listening skills**

  This entails focusing on the overall compliance your child is demonstrating rather than the specific behavior displayed. For example, at the end of the evening Mom may praise her children after she notices that they have put their coats away where they belong, made their lunches for school tomorrow, and put their dirty snack dishes in the sink. Furthermore, as noted in Chapter 4, it's essential to "catch," or attend to, your child's positive behavior, as attention is inherently reinforcing and clearly sends the message to "keep doing that."

7. *Follow through with what you say.*

If your child is a chronic non-listener, he may need more than just praise or other reinforcement to ensure that he complies with directives. He may need to experience a repercussion to comprehend the import of listening and adhering to directives.

But in order for these repercussions to be effective, there needs to be follow-through. Oftentimes, children's poor listening skills are the direct result of parents' failing to simply do what they've said. A parent may state that "we're leaving in five minutes" but linger an extra 30 minutes. They may say, "You're not going to have another playdate if . . ." but then schedule one later in the week. Parents need to be mindful of what they say. *If you can't or won't follow through, don't say it.* It undermines your authority and results in children feeling as though listening is optional. As you'll read in Chapter 6, following through with natural and logical consequences can be an extremely effective way to foster better listening.

Final Thoughts

As this chapter suggests, there is a complementary relationship between a nurturing communication style and the strategies that foster better listening. Their consistent use is likely to propagate an overall message of respect and high behavioral standards within the home—from the perspective of both the adult and the child. It's essential that parents role-model these principles in order to teach and reinforce their use in the children. Children will learn that parents are fair, supportive, consistent, and loving, and in return, they will respond by mirroring this type of communication. As you'll learn in subsequent chapters, this will serve as the foundation for understanding natural and logical consequences and coping with power struggles.

Key Points Discussed in Chapter 5

- Diana Baumrind (1967) described four primary parenting styles: authoritarian, permissive, uninvolved, and authoritative. Authoritative is believed to be the most beneficial to children's overall development.

- Authoritative parenting has several positive characteristics, including:
  - Balancing the need for rules with a responsiveness to emotion
  - Balancing the child's need to ask questions and make choices with the need to set high expectations and healthy boundaries
  - Reinforcing positive behavior
  - Being firm but not punitive
  - Administering clear, fair, and consistent consequences

(continued)

- Nurturing communication is characterized by respectful, empathic language; a warm, encouraging tone; and gentle and meaningful physical touch. Each of these is intended to convey to the child that he or she is valued, respected, and supported. To be effective, nurturing communication has to become part of the overall culture within your home, not just used selectively.

- The most common complaint heard from parents is that they feel their child does not listen or respond to directions.

- When a child doesn't listen, most of the time it's a performance deficit. The child can follow the directions, but he chooses not to. Modifying how you present information and directives can greatly enhance your child's motivation to listen.

- There are several other ways to enhance your child's listening skills:
  - Use proximity, refer to the child by name, and make eye contact.
  - Prioritize directions and keep them simple.
  - Tell children what TO do, not just what NOT to do.
  - Check for comprehension.
  - Use praise for each direction followed.
  - Follow through with what's stated.

- One of the consequences of transitioning from an ineffective style of communicating to a nurturing communication style is an immediate improvement in listening behavior.

Notes:

Chapter 6

Utilizing Natural vs. Logical Consequences and Coping with Power Struggles

By this point, we've talked about reinforcing positive behavior, adopting a nurturing communication style, and encouraging better listening. We've discussed how these variables will promote a culture of respect and goodwill in the home, resulting in the establishment of clear, age-appropriate expectations and a significant reduction in misbehavior.

In this chapter, we're first going to discuss how to administer natural and logical consequences and then examine several ways to cope with power struggles. As originally noted in Chapter 2, all behavior stems from the desire to have an internal need met. Once a behavior is displayed, there is a reaction, or consequence, that results from this behavior. This consequence may reinforce (encourage) or punish (discourage) the behavior. Our goal, of course, is to reinforce positive behavior so that it takes precedence over misbehavior.

Dr. Tara Egan's Behavioral Model

Natural Consequences

It's important to recognize that there are naturally occurring consequences to *every* behavior. Natural consequences can be positive or negative, depending on our choices. Some examples include:

If you don't get up on time for school, you'll miss the bus.

If you don't wash your clothes, you won't have any clean clothes to wear to school or work.

If you're kind to your peers, you'll make friends.

If you park too close to the car next to yours, your car might get scraped by someone else's door.

If you study, you're more likely to earn a good grade.

If you don't wear shoes, you might step on something sharp.

In these examples, there isn't a need to put extensive thought into the consequences, as they occur naturally. Oftentimes, however, parents interfere with the situation to the point that natural consequences cannot be experienced and learned from. Let's look back at the example listed above of the child who doesn't get up on time for school:

> **Natural consequences are outcomes that occur without interference from another person.**

Charlie, age nine, is in the fourth grade. He's been instructed to set his alarm and rise by 6:00 a.m. so he can catch the school bus at 6:45 a.m. Each morning, his mother opens his bedroom door at 6:05 a.m., calls out his name, and flips on his lights. Charlie typically buries his head under the covers. Every two or three minutes, Mom returns to Charlie's room and urges him to get up. By 6:15 a.m., she's typically raising her voice and shaking Charlie. When she gets to this point in their routine, Charlie knows that he needs to get up in order to make it to school on time. He finally rises, finds his breakfast already prepared by his mother, and eats it moments before he slips out the door to the bus stop.

In this scenario, a natural consequence of not setting an alarm might be that Charlie oversleeps.

A natural consequence of not getting up on time might be that Charlie doesn't have time to eat breakfast.

A natural consequence of not getting up on time might be that Charlie misses the school bus.

A natural consequence of missing the bus might be that Charlie has to find an alternate ride to school. Which will cause someone to consume the gas in their car. Which costs money. There is money in the jar on Charlie's bureau. (See where I'm going with this?)

Determining Natural Consequences

Because natural consequences occur without interference from someone else, they typically take less effort to predict. One way to anticipate a natural consequence is to think, "What would happen to *me* if I did this?" You are an adult, and presumably, you don't have a person in your life who is orchestrating consequences when you make poor choices. You just have to live with naturally occurring consequences (unless your spouse or boss bails you out all the time—if so, shame on them).

As parents, however, we often struggle to let natural consequences evolve to the point where they impact our children. As Chapter 5 suggests, this is particularly true for permissive parents, as they are reluctant to allow their child to suffer a physical, social, or emotional hardship even if it's an excellent opportunity for her to learn from her behavior. For many parents, however, it's not necessarily the distress of their child that bothers them, but the idea that allowing the occurrence of natural consequences may reflect poorly on their parenting abilities.

Consider the child who leaves her lunch box sitting on the counter as she leaves for school. A natural consequence of forgetting her lunch is that the child goes without lunch. However, the parent may ultimately decide to make a special trip to school to drop off the lunch because they fear that they will appear harsh, uncompassionate, or even neglectful in the eyes of their child's teachers if they allow their child to experience the consequences of their behavior. But the fact is, the child is much less likely to repeat this behavior if she experiences a few hunger pangs throughout the afternoon. Clearly, the price of learning this lesson in responsibility is relatively low.

When a parent is faced with the prospect of either allowing natural consequences to evolve or protecting a child from physical or emotional hardship, it may be helpful to ask the following questions:

1. Can the child be seriously hurt?

Of course, if the child can be seriously harmed emotionally or physically, then you may need to set aside natural consequences and consider logical consequences, to be discussed later in this chapter. An example: If your child misses the bus in the morning, it would be unwise to allow her to walk to school in the dark along a busy road.

2. **Am I allowing my decision to be influenced by my fear of being judged or misunderstood by others?**

If you're altering the trajectory of natural consequences because you're worried about the opinion of another, then you're probably letting a valuable learning opportunity escape unnecessarily. The example described above illustrates this.

3. **Does the natural consequence correlate enough with the child's behavior that the child will actually learn something?**

Sometimes natural consequences won't necessarily serve to discourage misbehavior, but will simply result in an unpleasant consequence for others. Consider the boy who fails to bring his toothbrush on vacation. The natural consequence is that he will have foul breath and be at greater risk for cavities. In actuality, however, everyone else will suffer more from his breath than he will, and his parents will ultimately be responsible for paying for his dental work. In this example, the boy would probably learn very little. Logical consequences, such as requiring him to use a portion of his spending money at the hotel convenience store, would probably be more effective at curbing this misbehavior.

Logical Consequences

If natural consequences are those that occur without outside interference, logical consequences are those that are determined by another person. However, logical consequences are closely related to the misbehavior.

For example, a natural consequence of a small child running out in the street is getting hit by a car. Clearly, this natural consequence is too severe to allow. In contrast, a logical consequence to a child running out into the street may be that he has to play inside for the remainder of the afternoon or he has to remain in the fenced-in backyard.

A natural consequence of leaving your handheld video game on a table in a restaurant is that someone takes it or it gets thrown away. A logical consequence is that when you retrieve it, you lose the privilege of taking it outside of the house.

As illustrated by the above examples, logical consequences are most appropriate to use when the natural consequence is too severe, unethical, or is going to take an extended period of time to result in a learning opportunity (for example, waiting for your high schooler to oversleep for 20 days may be excessive when it comes to learning the consequences of not attending school).

Here are some examples of logical consequences:

Jeremy, age six, is very active while he's watching television. He stands, jumps, and rolls on the couch, smashing the cushions and causing the couch to give an alarming creak. While the natural consequence is that the couch will get ruined, his mother opts to impart logical consequences in hopes of preserving the couch. Now, after one warning, Jeremy is asked to sit his bottom on the floor while watching television. His mother cheerfully states, "If he can't sit on the couch appropriately, then he won't be permitted to sit on it at all. If he'd like to sit while watching television, he can sit on the floor." Turns out, watching television when one isn't permitted to use the couch is not fun.

Mya, age two, always throws her food off of her high chair tray while she's eating. It makes a huge mess and gets her mother very frustrated. A natural consequence of throwing food on the floor is that all the food is gone within a few moments and Mya is forced to go hungry. A logical consequence, imparted by her mother, is that Mya is asked to get down and pick up each piece of food on the floor. Only when Mya picks them up is she permitted to have more food. After several instances of climbing down, picking up all the food, and climbing back into her chair, Mya decides it's not worth the time and effort to throw food.

In order to decide upon an appropriate logical consequence, the parent needs to tie the original misbehavior to the consequence. It may help to ask, "Does this make sense? Are the behavior and the consequence related?" For example, it doesn't make sense when a child who rips all the pages out of a library book is punished by not being permitted to ride his bike later in the day. After all, books and bike riding aren't necessarily related. But requiring the boy to donate several of his books to the library or earn money to pay for the damaged book may be a more meaningful logical consequence.

Intrinsic and Extrinsic Motivation Revisited

We'd like to think that allowing a child to experience natural or logical consequences will result in a modification of their behavior so that future decision making is more productive (from our perspective, at least). Ideally, a child will experience the consequences, decide he values the consequences that result from engaging in positive behavior, and become intrinsically motivated to behave in a positive manner. For example, a child who learns from natural consequences that teasing his peers makes him disliked may eventually alter his behavior and experience pride at being liked and respected. As noted in Chapter 4, pride is an intrinsic motivator and serves as a catalyst for future behavior.

However, sometimes the natural or logical consequence is not actually a deterrent for a child. Intrinsic motivation may never develop, requiring motivation by extrinsic factors, such as money, praise, or privileges. For example, poor school attendance, study habits, and homework completion may result in a child failing her high school courses. However, this student may be immune to this natural consequence, as graduating from high school isn't a priority. Similarly, failing to wash clothing will eventually result in a person only having dirty clothes to wear. However, some people don't value hygiene or worry about other people's perceptions of them.

In these scenarios, the desired behavior has to be motivated via a consequence unrelated to the misbehavior. For example, if the child fails to complete his school responsibilities, he may lose the privilege of using his cell phone. If a child refuses to do her laundry, she may be denied the opportunity to spend time with friends. This strays from the goal of inspiring intrinsic motivation via the use of natural or logical consequences, yet it's sometimes necessary. Choosing the appropriate extrinsic motivator will be essential to fostering motivation. The reader may wish to refer back to Chapter 4 to revisit the discussion about the types of reinforcement that may be most effective for your child.

Coping with Power Struggles

Claire, age four, has always struggled at bedtime. After her parents tuck her into bed at 8:00 p.m., she typically leaves her room about ten minutes later and sits at the top of the stairs. From this spot, she can see the television. When her parents prompt her to go back to bed, she reports that she needs to use the bathroom. Or get a sip of water. Or she's had a bad dream. Or she's scared of a noise she heard outside. Or she's too hot. Or too cold. Each time her parents return Claire to her bed, explaining that she needs to get some rest prior to preschool tomorrow, Claire creeps out of her room again a few minutes later. Sometimes this dance occurs up to seven or eight times per night until Claire finally falls asleep at approximately 10:30 p.m.

If you recall from Chapter 2, insufficient sleep is associated with a variety of issues, including poor coping, characteristics associated with ADHD, and increased aggressive and defiant behavior. Therefore, Claire's parents are justified in feeling concerned. Initially, Claire's parents first attempt to address her troublesome bedtime behavior by establishing and adhering to a structured nighttime routine, giving Claire plenty of advance warning

> **A power struggle is a battle between two people or groups, both of whom are trying to establish dominance in the relationship.**

as bedtime approaches and reinforcing positive behavior such as Claire's putting on her pajamas without complaint. In addition, they allow natural consequences to take effect, such as allowing Claire to experience the fatigue and irritability associated with a lack of sleep (rather than allowing her to take an excessively long nap during the day, for example). They also impart logical consequences, such as putting Claire to bed significantly earlier so that she has plenty of time to engage in her stalling tactics before 8:00 p.m. After these strategies prove to be ineffective, however, Claire's parents acknowledge that they are firmly embroiled in a power struggle.

Dr. Tara Egan's Behavioral Model

A power struggle can occur between a parent and a child when the child is consistently sent the message that they have decision-making power over choices that should be made by an adult. In the above example, Claire appears to feel as though she is the authority on 1) when bedtime occurs and 2) whether or not she has to remain in her bedroom after her parents say goodnight. Clearly, these are parental decisions, as Claire's parents' role is to offer guidance, protect Claire's health and safety, and set boundaries that are fair, clear, and respectful. Parents can do this by using nurturing communication to avoid straying into an authoritarian parenting style that resorts to using harsh words or a domineering attitude. Ideally, parents would prevent power struggles using the strategies described in the previous chapters, such as "catching" their child behaving, using nurturing communication, and presenting directions in a manner that encourages better listening. If power struggles are avoided, then there is no competition. There is simply a natural order of things—the parent is the guiding adult who respectfully establishes clear, fair, and consistent boundaries. The child, in response, is able to benefit from her parents' guidance without feeling either placated, dominated, or as if her emotions are insignificant.

The top three situations that often lead to a power struggle include:
- **Morning routine**
- **Mealtimes**
- **Bedtime**

The earlier that parents are able to identify a potential power struggle, the more likely they are to eliminate the source of the potential argument. After all, if an argument never escalates, then a power struggle about that issue cannot ensue. Most of the time, this can be accomplished by imparting logical consequences.

Scenario	Caught in a Power Struggle	Elimination of a Potential Power Struggle via Logical Consequences
Your child always throws his books on the floor and then whines incessantly for you to reach back and retrieve them while you're driving.	You keep picking them up.	You stop allowing books in the car.
Your child won't surrender the Nintendo Wii remote to his friend during a playdate and arguments ensue.	You keep serving as the mediator as they continue to argue.	You make the Nintendo Wii off-limits during playdates.
It's impossible to pry your child away from the television to start his homework.	You keep nagging or threatening him until he gets started.	You don't permit the television to be turned on after school until homework is completed.

As the above scenarios illustrate, imparting a logical consequence can effectively stop power struggles before they escalate.

However, for those occasions when power struggles cannot be prevented, the following suggestions may be helpful.

Top Ten Tips to Avoid Power Struggles

1. *Pick your battles.*

As parents, we have days that seem to consist primarily of scolding, giving directives, correcting, or reminding. Each activity appears to be accompanied by an argument, resistance, or negotiation.

But sometimes, the issue isn't important enough to warrant a battle. While the topic being debated may be excruciatingly important to your child, your "stake" in the decision may be minimal. So let it go. Oftentimes, as parents, we get into a habit of giving directives and guidance even when they're not warranted. This is closely related to the discussion from Chapter 3, in which parents are encouraged to prioritize their behavioral expectations rather than burden the child with demands that, upon inspection, aren't particularly valued.

> Parents who are confident in their decision-making skills and ability to parent effectively are less likely to engage in power struggles with their children.

Sometimes it's important to have an inner conversation with yourself that goes something like this: "Tara, do you really care if your daughter has cleaned up her room prior to Grandma coming to visit? After all, they're just going to get out all the toys again anyway. Grandma knows I keep a clean house; she's not going to judge me for having some toys scattered around."

Here's another example of a battle not worth fighting:

Mom: Justin, put on your coat. It's time to go.

Justin: No, I don't want to wear my coat.

Mom: It's cold out, buddy. Put it on so we can pick up your sister from school.

Justin: I hate my coat. I can't get it zipped.

Mom: I'll zip it for you. Put it on.

Justin: No, I'm not cold. I don't want to wear it.

Mom: You're going to get cold and then you're going to complain. Put it on. I'm not telling you again.

Justin: I won't be cold. I won't complain.

Mom: You will be cold. It's 42 degrees out. It's supposed to snow later. Put it on.

Justin: It's not snowing now. I'm warm now. Actually, I'm hot now.

Mom: For goodness sake! You are not hot! Put on the coat! Stop arguing about everything!

As you can see, this conversation could go on for a while. Instead, consider this:

Mom: Justin, put on your coat. It's time to go.

Justin: No, I don't want to wear my coat.

Mom: Okay. Just bring it with you in case you need it.

Justin: Okay.

In your quest to be recognized as the person of authority in a given circumstance, it's important to set a worthy goal. But how do you know if it's something that can be "let go"? While ultimately this decision is unique to each situation, you may want to ask yourself the following questions:

1. Does it impact the safety of my child?

2. Is this a behavior to which I'm absolutely opposed and don't want to see repeated (remember in Chapter 1 when we stated the theme of "Don't let your child do today what you don't want them do tomorrow")?

3. Do I *really* care about this?

If the answer to any of these is "yes," then this behavior should be prioritized. If you "let it go," you may simply be giving in to your child's demands due to fatigue or frustration. Power struggles are most likely to occur if children sense that they get a "vote" as to whether they have to follow a particular directive. If given that impression, they will simply keep insisting until you surrender your stance and permit them to do what they want. However, if you prioritize your behavioral expectations, make it clear that you're going maintain your decision, and administer the consequences you've originally stated, they'll learn that engaging in a power struggle is fruitless.

2. Offer two acceptable choices. . .sometimes.

In the popular media, much is publicized about giving your child choices. I think this is one of the most widely circulated recommendations in the history of parenting advice. The benefits of permitting your child to participate in decision making are three-fold:

- The child feels more in control of his environment.

- When a child participates in decision making, he feels more invested in the outcome. When a child feels more invested in the outcome, he will put more time and effort into the behavior that will elicit the outcome he wants.

- The child is permitted to make a choice and then experience the consequence of that choice. If she has made a good choice, the positive outcome should reinforce that type of decision making. If she has made a poor choice, the negative outcome presumably results in a change in her decision-making process.

Parents, however, often spend their entire day giving their child choices. After a while, this can feel less like giving choices and more like constant negotiation. Allowing a child to make too many choices can backfire, as all children benefit from some boundaries or general expectations. If you permit the child to make 1) too many choices or 2) choices that are not age-appropriate, then she may feel overwhelmed, causing her to experience anxiety, indecisiveness, or just overall mental fatigue.

Therefore, choices should be:

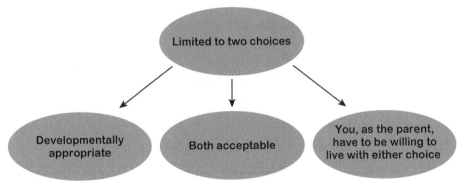

Limited Choices

For example, don't ask a four-year-old to decide her own punishment for misbehaving. Don't ask her to decide where you're going on your summer vacation. Don't ask her to decide on a name for her baby brother (that leads to a discussion about why "Superman," "Twist," or "Princess Aurora" are not really baby-friendly names). You're giving her too much responsibility, and she doesn't have the tools to make an appropriate decision. Instead, ask her which sneakers she wants to wear today, which snack might be the most appealing, or which television show she would like to watch while Dad is preparing dinner.

3. *Adhere to your decisions.*

Once we've prioritized our behavioral expectations and expressed them using a nurturing communication style, it's important to adhere to these decisions. If you've indicated that your child must complete his homework prior to turning on the television, it's important that you respectfully express this expectation and remain consistent with your stance.

> Parents often report experiencing guilt when they say "no" to their child. This, in turn, often results in their retracting the initial decision.

Oftentimes, parents will describe themselves as pushovers. A mom or dad will say, "I tell him no, but then he'll convince me to do it differently." Or, "I'll tell her what I've decided, and she'll talk me out of it." While I applaud parents who attempt to factor in their child's opinions and preferences, there's a difference between mindfully seeking your child's thoughts and opinions about an issue and capitulating after being badgered incessantly. Sometimes the situation requires a parent simply to make a decision and gently and consistently enforce it through the use of a nurturing communication style.

How and When to Factor in Your Child's Opinion

As noted earlier in this chapter, there are times when we want to give our child choices or factor in his or her opinion. Let's examine what you should consider when deciding whether it's appropriate to solicit a child's opinion.

First, you need to determine whether your child is even developmentally mature enough to render an opinion about the particular issue. Asking a small child (such as a child between the ages of two and seven years old) her opinion about food, clothing choices, or nonessential activities or entertainment may be appropriate. Asking an older child (over seven years) his opinion about preferred activities, school tasks, and common social issues may be appropriate. You need to consider your child's level of maturity and ability to make an informed, reasonable decision.

Second, you need to evaluate whether the child deserves to have her opinion considered. More specifically, consider whether your child has made her request in a respectful way. If she has done so in an abrasive or disrespectful manner, then altering your decision based on her request will simply reinforce her offensive behavior, making it more likely that she will use a similar tone in the future.

Consider the following example:

Mom (leaving swim class with her son): Hey, Luke, I was thinking we should go to Marcos Pizza for dinner tonight. What do you think? Are you in the mood for pizza?

Luke (regular tone of voice): No, Mom. I want chicken fingers. Can we get chicken fingers?

Mom: Can you ask me more nicely?

Luke: Can we get chicken fingers. . .please?

Mom: Okay, sounds good.

In this scenario, Luke's opinion is solicited, and he responds in a respectful tone. By asking Luke's opinion, his mother is prepared to consider his response. When he responds respectfully and reasonably, she is able to reinforce his request by granting it, thereby increasing the likelihood that he will respond similarly next time.

Notice that Mom:

- Asks his opinion only when she is prepared to listen to it and consider it (although she is not obligated to agree with him)

- Asks his opinion regarding an age-appropriate question (meal preference)

- Sets the expectation that he answer her questions in a respectful manner

But what happens if a parent gives a child advance notice and he still responds in a demanding, disrespectful tone?

Mom (as they're leaving swim class): Hey, Luke, I was thinking we should go to Marcos Pizza for dinner tonight. What do you think? Are you in the mood for pizza?

Luke (in a whiny, plaintive tone): No, Mom. I don't want pizza! I want chicken fingers! Let's go somewhere else!

Mom (calmly): I would like you to answer my question in a nicer tone of voice, Luke. What would you like to do for dinner?

Luke (demanding): I want chicken fingers! I hate pizza! I'm not eating pizza!

Mom: I'm not going to take someone to a restaurant who cannot speak to me in a nice way. We'll eat something at home tonight and save our trip to a restaurant for another day.

Luke, disappointed, cries and screams the entire way home while Mom ignores him (providing absolutely no reinforcement).

Note that this example demonstrates several of the principles outlined in prior chapters. As we learned in Chapter 3, Mom recognizes that persisting with her decision to visit a restaurant while accompanied by a whiny, argumentative child would be completely frustrating. She "knows her limits" and avoids the further progression of the power struggle by withdrawing all attention to Luke's misbehavior. In addition, as recommended in Chapter 4, which notes that children must not be simply told what not to do but must be taught the appropriate behavior, best practice requires that Mom wait until Luke calms down and then offer him several examples of appropriate ways he could have expressed his preference for chicken fingers.

4. *Always clearly describe the potential consequences of misbehavior and adhere to them.*

Upon first glance, this recommendation may appear to mirror number 3, which states that you must adhere to the initial decision you've made about a specific situation. However, this tip refers to 1) the necessity of giving advance notice of potential consequences and 2) the need to follow through with the consequences you've articulated.

Jennifer, mother to Henry, age seven:

Henry: Mom, can I have a snack?

Mom: Sure. You can have grapes and one chocolate chip cookie.

Henry (takes the grapes offered and grabs a cookie from the plate on the counter): Thanks.

Mom: Eat up and then we're going to start your homework.

Henry (grabs another cookie): Can I have another cookie?

Mom: No, you've already had one.

Henry: Please?

Mom: Nope. Put it back or you'll forfeit your dessert after dinner. You choose.

Henry (eats another cookie): Okay.

After dinner, Henry reaches for a cookie.

Mom: Henry, you already had two cookies after school. You can have some fruit or some yogurt if you'd like something else.

Henry: Mom! I just want one more! Please?

Mom: No, Henry. I told you that if you ate two cookies after school, you wouldn't be able to eat any more after dinner. Your choice is to pick out something healthy or excuse yourself from the table.

In this example, notice that Mom clearly describes the consequences of Henry eating the extra cookie after school and then adheres to them later in the evening. Even though it may have been easier simply to give in to Henry's desire to have one more cookie, giving in to a power struggle is likely to increase the probability that a power struggle will occur in the future. From the child's perspective, it "worked." Remaining consistent with a previously stated consequence can be very difficult for parents, but it is an extremely effective strategy.

5. Factor in sensory needs.

As discussed in Chapter 3, sometimes misbehavior can be more accurately described as a sensory need, a need that evolves from a child's struggle to process sensory information (information collected through a child's sense of touch, smell, sight, hearing, or taste). If you're getting into a power struggle with your child, consider whether his battle was instigated by his clumsy attempt to meet a sensory need.

> What does a "sensory need" refer to? When a child is having trouble processing information that is related to one of his senses: hearing, vision, taste, touch, or smell.

For example, Christine, mother of Jacob, a first grader, is extremely frustrated by Jacob's refusal to participate in basketball practice. At home, he shoots baskets for hours by himself or with one or two of his friends. But when he is expected to participate during practice, he whines, complains of physical symptoms, and expresses a desire to leave early. After observing Jacob in both settings, I am able to see that this is a sensory issue. During practice, all eight members of the team are given their own ball to use. Eight noisy balls pounding on the indoor gym floor is deafening, and Jacob physically recoils and tries to escape with a myriad of excuses when the dribbling begins. After Jacob switches to a team that plays on an outdoor, paved basketball court, resulting in considerably less noise and chaos, he is able to take more pleasure in the sport.

If parents determine that misbehavior is actually triggered by a sensory issue, they can make modifications to their child's environment in order to better support them. Refer back to Chapter 2 for more specific tips about how to address these issues.

6. *To chase or not to chase. . .*

"Chasing" can be defined as any time you have to physically assist your child to follow a directive you've just provided. Chasing consists of three parts:

a. Giving a verbal direction

b. Your child ignoring or blatantly defying your directive

c. Needing to physically guide your child to follow your directive

Some examples of chasing may include:

Scenario 1: How silly do you feel when you're sitting in a waiting room and you realize that your five-year-old son has pilfered a piece of candy out of your purse 45 minutes before dinner? You tell him to give it back, rise out of your seat, and chase him around the waiting room, getting more frustrated and embarrassed as he eludes your grasp. Finally, you pull him out from under a chair by his legs. Caught, he begins crying, and you forcibly pry his hand open to retrieve the candy. You're out of breath and the focus of attention. Your son is clearly upset and has learned nothing from the experience.

Scenario 2: You're at a friend's house with your three-year-old daughter, who is playing with your friend's children. It's time to leave. You instruct her to put on her coat and shoes. She resists, yelling, "No! I want to stay and play!" After giving her two prompts, you inform your friend that you're about to have a "parenting moment." You gather your purse, her coat, and her shoes. You enter the playroom, scoop her up off the floor, and carry her to the car. She screams. You ignore her, buckle her into her car seat, and drive home.

In the first scenario, you "chased" in an attempt to "win" the power struggle by preventing your son from eating the candy. All this did was result in the escalation of the power struggle. In the second scenario, you "chased" your daughter by physically insisting that she leave the playdate.

What's the difference? How do you know whether to chase or not chase?

Consider the following:

a. Is your child younger than three and/or does your child struggle to understand language? Then chasing is permitted. If they're actually running from you, then they're too small to get very far, and you'll send a clear message if you halt the power struggle immediately and leave the premises. If you have to chase, realize that your child needs consequences for two misbehaviors: 1) not following your initial direction (such as giving back the piece of candy) and 2) running from you. If you've had to chase, the "running" behavior is probably the misbehavior to prioritize.

b. Is your child older than three and able to understand language? If yes, then don't chase. You child will run just fast enough to elude you (i.e., embarrass you), and you'll fare better if you simply state the consequences for not following your directions and adhere to them (for example, you may say, "If you don't give me back the piece of candy you took from my purse, then you may not eat the Goldfish® crackers that the nurse will give you after your appointment").

c. Is your child *actually* running from you, or is he physically not moving? If he's *not* actually moving and is simply disobeying your directive, then it's okay to physically guide him if needed. An example of this may be taking a toy that is being misused out of his hand, taking him by the hand to guide him back to his bed, or carrying him out to the car after he's just made a scene in a restaurant.

d. Is safety a concern? If your child is running in a parking lot or holding something dangerous, like scissors, you will have no choice but to chase.

Remember, the act of chasing a child can be reinforcing for a child, as it's rewarding to see a parent get upset and out of breath. If you remain calm and clearly state the consequences of her misbehavior (and adhere to them), she'll realize that running from you (or otherwise defying you) doesn't get 1) her attention or 2) you to "cave in" to the misbehavior.

7. Remember that your child is not your friend.

It's very difficult to set an authoritative tone with your child if you haven't established a relationship that identifies you, the parent, as the authority figure. Many parents develop a relationship with their child that more closely mirrors that of a friendship, in which both the child and the parent have equal decision-making power. As we discussed in Chapter 5, this is a characteristic most associated with permissive parenting.

Treating your child like a friend is naturally going to foster power struggles, as the line between "parent" and "child" will be blurred. Children are not the peers of adults; they are to be guided, protected, and nurtured by the parent. Children need to be sent the message that:

- You, the parent, are the decision maker.
- You are, in general, a good decision maker (consistent, fair, and respectful).
- Your decisions are to be respected.
- If your behavioral expectations are not adhered to, there will be (fair and respectful) consequences.

In turn, you need to send yourself the following message:

- You, the parent, are the decision maker.
- You are, in general, a good decision maker (consistent, fair, and respectful).
- Your decisions are to be respected and adhered to.
- Your decisions are made to guide your child and protect his best interests. While it's important to be sensitive to your child's emotions, it's inevitable that children are going to occasionally experience anger, frustration, and disappointment. Sometimes these negative feelings are unavoidable, as not all of life's lessons are enjoyable to learn.

8. Make sure your child knows what to expect.

Power struggles can frequently be avoided if the child knows what to expect. If you recall, we spoke in-depth about the benefits of advance warnings and clear expectations in Chapter 3. When we ask a child to transition from one activity to the next with 1) little advance warning, or 2) unclear expectations, misbehavior is more likely to occur.

Here's a scenario:

Mom: Caleb, do you want to go draw with chalk on the driveway?

Caleb: Yeah!

Mom: Okay, let's go outside. But remember, we have to leave in 20 minutes to pick up your sister from school.

Caleb: Okay.

(They draw together for about 10 minutes.)

Mom: In about two minutes, we're going to start cleaning up the chalk. We need to wash our hands and get in the car so we aren't late picking up your sister. Do you understand, Caleb? We're going to be all done with this in a minute.

Caleb: Yes.

Mom: Okay, pick one last piece of chalk. Let's draw one last quick picture and then we'll put this chalk away. Look, I'm drawing an elephant.

Caleb: I'm drawing a monster.

Mom: Very scary! Here, stick that piece of chalk in the box. Good! Now, let's go wash our hands. My hands are so dusty. Thank you so much, Caleb, for being such a good listener. We'll show your sister your picture when we get home.

If you'll notice, in this scenario:

- Mom set the behavioral expectation at the beginning of the activity. (*We will be using chalk on the driveway. We will use it for only 20 minutes.*)

- She checked for comprehension to make sure that Caleb understood the expectation. She gave him an advance warning so he could mentally and physically prepare himself for the transition. (*In two minutes, we will clean up the chalk and go to pick up your sister.*)

- She assisted him with the actual transition. (*Let's draw one last picture and put that piece of chalk away.*)

- She praised him for complying. (*Thank you so much, Caleb, for being such a good listener. We'll show your sister your picture when we get home.*)

9. Co-parent effectively so that your child will not exploit your indecision and disharmony.

Whether you are married, divorced, or simply sharing care of your child with a family member or a child care provider, it's important to have consistent expectations. This is most relevant for very young children, as younger children are less able to understand the nuances between caregivers and respond accordingly. If the child, when with one parent, learns that engaging in power struggles leads to capitulation, he's more likely to try that strategy with the other parent or another caregiver. Co-parenting effectively doesn't require parents to parent in an identical manner (although both parents should strive to use a nurturing communication style). It does, however, suggest that both parents need to have an equally developed level of authority. If all caregivers set age-appropriate boundaries, power struggles will be reduced, even those instigated by the most strong-willed child.

10. *Recognize the impact of your reaction to the power struggle.*

As noted elsewhere in this book, all attention is inherently reinforcing. Therefore, if you respond to a power struggle with attention (even if it's negative attention, such as scolding), you're increasing the likelihood that it will occur again. Therefore, if you find yourself in a power struggle with your child, attempt to disengage with your child.

Daniel and his daughter Mya (age seven) are playing a board game. Partway through the game, Mya realizes that her dad is about to win. Quickly, she takes an extra card off the deck and slips it into her handful of cards. Daniel notices.

Dad: Mya, you need to play fairly. Put the card back.

Mya: I didn't take a card, Daddy.

Dad: Yes, you did. I saw you take it. If you don't play by the rules, that's cheating.

Mya: No, I didn't!

Dad (he grasps her deck of cards and gently thumbs through it): Yes, you did.

Mya: I did not!

Dad (recognizing that they are in a power struggle): We'll play later when you're ready to play by the rules. (He says this calmly, then quietly tucks the pieces of the game back in the box and leaves the table. Mya, surprised, begins to cry.)

In this situation, note that Daniel:

- Doesn't argue with Mya
- Doesn't prolong the interaction (minimizing the attention that Mya receives for her misbehavior)
- Remains calm and matter-of-fact
- Simply ends the dialogue, sending a clear message that he is no longer going to interact with her while she is attempting to engage in a power struggle

Final Thoughts

Power struggles are among the most common and frustrating type of interactions that you can have with your child. Power struggles with your child can be exhausting, may undermine your confidence as a parent, and may compel you to lower your behavioral expectations by "giving in." However, recognizing and practicing the above strategies can reduce their frequency, minimize their impact when they do occur, and encourage harmony within the home.

Key Points Discussed in Chapter 6

- Natural consequences are outcomes that occur without interference from another person. In contrast, logical consequences are outcomes that are determined by another person, although the consequences are closely related to the misbehavior.

- In order to determine whether something is a natural consequence, it may help to consider, "What would happen to me, an adult, if I behaved this way?"

- Logical consequences are most appropriate to use when natural consequences are too severe, unethical, or can't be realized for an excessive amount of time.

- Although the hope is that natural and logical consequences will lead to intrinsically motivated positive behavior, sometimes this isn't successful because the child doesn't place a high enough value on the outcome. In this situation, the consequences may have to be manipulated so that a child is motivated extrinsically.

- A power struggle is a battle between two people or groups, both of whom are trying to establish dominance in the relationship. In the parent-child relationship, power struggles ensue when the child is consistently sent the message that he or she has decision-making power over choices that should be made by an adult.

- The best way to cope with power struggles is to prevent them.

- The following are 10 tips for avoiding power struggles:
  1. Pick your battles.
  2. Offer two acceptable choices. Make sure they're developmentally appropriate, and make sure you can live with either one.
  3. Adhere to your decisions. However, it may be appropriate to factor in your child's opinion about minor issues if he demonstrates the ability to make requests in a calm, respectful manner.
  4. Always clearly describe the potential consequences of misbehavior and adhere to them.
  5. Factor in sensory needs.
  6. Chase only if your child is younger than three and/or struggles to understand language, or if it's a safety issue. The rest of the time, simply state the consequences of defiance and adhere to them.
  7. Remember that your child is not your friend.
  8. Make sure your child knows what to expect.
  9. Co-parent effectively so that your child will not exploit your indecision and disharmony.
  10. Recognize the role of your reaction to the power struggle.

Chapter 7

Understanding and Navigating Temper Outbursts

Every new parent is warned that temper outbursts are coming. More experienced parents feel compelled to share the details of their child's worst moments with all the expression and story-telling ability of a group of Boy Scouts around a campfire. To listen to their stories, you'd think that their child's head could spin around 360 degrees and their scream could rival that of an angry monkey. Or that the child had developed the ability to lift cars and throw bricks in their rage. Or that the outburst lasted so long into the night that the parent was convinced that vampire blood coursed through the child's veins. And their stories inevitably involve the outburst occurring in the worst setting possible—at Grandma's funeral, at the picnic hosted by their employer, or during baby brother's baptism.

As a new parent with an infant sleeping peacefully in her carrier, you chuckle because of course your child won't act that way.

And then the first temper outburst occurs. This one may be rather amusing. Your toddler, enraged because you tell him that he can't eat the entire contents of your cosmetic bag, screams and weeps enormous tears as he frantically reaches for the purse you took away and placed on the counter. You may solve it by

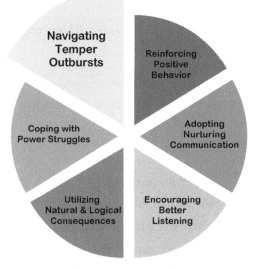

Dr. Tara Egan's Behavioral Model

distracting him with a snack, favorite toy, or a silly dance around the kitchen. You may give in and let him play with a large plastic comb and an empty zippered pouch. You may just ignore him until he stops. Regardless, the outburst is trifling compared to the horror stories you've heard.

But the twentieth outburst, conducted in a grocery store somewhere between the produce department and the bread aisle, may be loud and humiliating. Your daughter may screech, "I hate you, Mommy! You're hurting me!" as you try to place her thrashing body in the seat in the shopping cart. She may deliberately wet herself. She may smack you in the face. Strangers stare and someone offers a completely useless comment such as, "I think she's really mad right now." Angry and tired of being gawked at by disapproving patrons, you abandon the cart in the aisle and march your daughter out to the car. You may be shaking with disbelief and shocked at the suddenness of it. You may scold her, only to regret your words later when she is calm and complacently eating her dinner.

What Is a Temper Outburst?

Traditional temper outbursts can be defined by a complete loss of emotional control by the child. Unfortunately, they are all too often accompanied by a complete breakdown of emotional control in the parent. This type of behavior is most likely to occur between the ages of one and four years.

Temper outbursts are expressed differently by each child, but your child may engage in one or more of the following behaviors while having an outburst:

Scream	Hit	Beg or plead	Throw themselves on floor
Cry	Kick	Wet or soil themselves	Bang their head against hard surface
Throw objects	Bite	Hold their breath	Take off all their clothes
Make threats	Scratch	Run away from area	Make gagging sounds

As exhausting as temper outbursts can be—for both parent and child—they are a typical part of children's development. All children have outbursts, although not all outbursts look identical. Outbursts may be externalized and present as loud and theatrical. In contrast, they may be internalized, with quiet tears or physical or emotional withdrawal. Some children's temperaments are more conducive to outbursts than those of other children. Children who are strong-willed, quick to cry, and more likely to express themselves physically are prone to have temper outbursts with increased frequency. And oftentimes, their outbursts last longer.

How Temper Outbursts Evolve with Age

By the time the child has reached school-age, the "traditional" temper outbursts displayed by toddlers and preschool-age children should be relatively rare, replaced by more mature forms of emotional expression. Emotional expression by older children may take the form of the following:

Pouting	Withdrawing
Slamming doors	Crying
Yelling/defiant words	Hitting siblings

It is likely to be elicited when a child feels particularly angry, helpless, or disappointed. After all, a seven-year-old who just learned that her best friend's birthday party was cancelled due to illness is unlikely to have the self-control to cope without a certain measure of tears and emotional angst.

Most notably, the emotional outbursts of older children are less likely to take place in public, as the social principles of peer pressure and peer acceptance are developing. By the age of six or seven years old, children are likely to have the social awareness that kicking and screaming in public is inappropriate and embarrassing both for their parents and themselves (let's be honest—they care more about themselves).

Why Children Have Temper Outbursts

1. *Children don't have the language skills to communicate their wants and needs in a persuasive, drama-free manner.*

Small children struggle to identify their emotions. Their ability to label emotions is rather simple, consisting of phrases such as, "I feel mad," "I feel sad," or "I feel happy." They don't have the developmental ability and experience to identify more complicated emotions, such as frustration, betrayal, loneliness, fear, or feeling misunderstood. For example, when a parent turns off the television set with (as perceived by the child) little warning, the child is not able to say, "Listen, Mom. There are about four minutes left in this program, and I'd really like to finish it. I realize that you need me to get ready for school, and I'm aware of its importance, but I'd like you to respect that this television show is very compelling, and I will probably think about it for hours if I'm not permitted to see the ending." (Wouldn't that be nice if your child could say that? Wouldn't you be likely to accommodate such a nicely put, reasonable request? Let's all take a moment and recognize that many *adults* can't communicate this effectively, let alone a small child.) No, the child simply reacts by bursting into tears, screaming, "That's not fair!" and "You're mean!" and reaching for the remote control to turn the television back on. This scenario is likely to end with more yelling and the removal of television privileges.

2. Children don't have well-developed frustration tolerance or impulse control.

When children are angry, frustrated, or disappointed, they don't have the internal mechanism that says, "Don't freak out. Calm down." So when a four-year-old is stymied during his clumsy attempt to build a fighter jet out of LEGO® blocks, he is more likely to react by throwing LEGO® pieces, crying, and shouting. They can't identify the warning signals that occur prior to their outburst—such as the feeling of rising frustration—in order to quickly problem-solve to avoid an outburst. Older children and adults typically recognize the limits of their frustration tolerance and learn to cope with emotional expression that is less severe—walking away, saying a juicy curse word under their breath, or transferring their anger to the manufacturer of the uncooperative item.

> It's important to remember that temper outbursts come from feelings and feelings are okay. It's how we deal with our feelings—the behavior that results from them—that's relevant. We want our children to manage their feelings in a healthy, productive way.

3. Children may be searching for autonomy or a sense of control over their environment.

Like all of us, children want to engage in activities that they find enjoyable or satisfying in some way. They want to make their own choices, implement their ideas, and impart a sense of order and boundaries within their environment. In order to do this in the manner they prefer, they need to have a sense of freedom and control. As parents, we often recognize when a child isn't ready to be independent (although sometimes we don't realize this, and we hover unnecessarily). But the child may feel ready—or at least feel ready to try—and either they 1) have a temper outburst because they don't feel you're giving them the autonomy they deserve and desire, or 2) you've given them the autonomy, but their skill level isn't developed enough to handle the newfound responsibility as smoothly as the child anticipated.

4. *Children have learned that it's a successful strategy to get what they want.*

As we discussed in Chapter 2, the behavior that is most likely to recur is the one that is reinforced. Therefore, if a temper outburst is reinforced—even negatively reinforced—then it is more likely to recur. And any time a child has an outburst and it results in an experience that is even minimally reinforcing, you've basically sent your child the message that 1) temper outbursts are okay and 2) temper outbursts work. Once you've sent this message, hold onto your hats, Mom and Dad. You're in for a bumpy ride.

The Seven Stages of a Temper Outburst for a Child

The noise, aggression, and general disruption that accompany a temper outburst can all blur into a period of awfulness and cacophony that doesn't appear to have a pattern or make sense. In actuality, however, a child's outburst, when examined closely, progresses through a series of stages. They are as follows:

Anatomy of a Tantrum: The Child

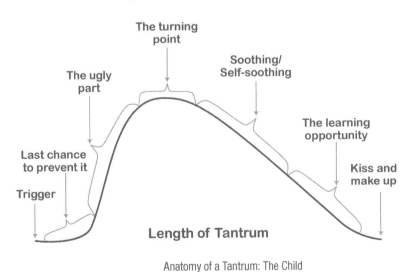

Anatomy of a Tantrum: The Child

The Role of Parents During Temper Outbursts

When discussing temper outbursts, we tend to focus on the *child's* experience within the outburst—their emotional upheaval, their misbehavior, and the progression from out-of-control behavior to a calm demeanor.

However, throughout a temper outburst, the parent also progresses through a series of stages. After all, watching your child experience extreme emotional distress is upsetting, particularly if the reason for their angst is easily relatable. Having an increased awareness of what you, as the parent, are probably experiencing may help you cope with the outburst in a manner that balances both your child's needs and your own.

The Seven Stages of a Temper Outburst for a Parent

These are the stages that the parent progresses through as the child's outburst is occurring:

Anatomy of a Tantrum: The Parent

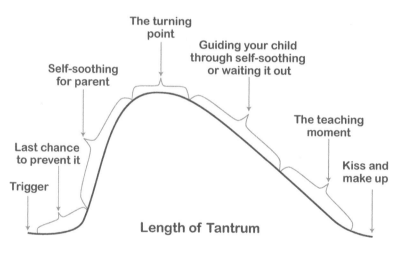

Anatomy of a Tantrum: The Parent

As you'll notice, the primary stages that are different for the parent and the child are the third and sixth stages.

The Trigger

The trigger, as one would imagine, is the event that precipitates the outburst. It's the factor that causes—or at minimum *contributes to*—an emotional outburst. There are two kinds of triggers: slow triggers and fast triggers.

Slow Triggers

Slow triggers are factors that increase the likelihood of an outburst occurring. They contribute to the emotional build-up that precedes the outburst. Think about when you, an adult, have an emotional outburst. Maybe you wake up late for work. Maybe you are out of coffee. Maybe you get in an argument with your spouse or are given an unpleasant task at work. Basically, the various components of your day contribute to a lousy mood that frays your patience or otherwise increases your sensitivity to negative events. Finally, when you get home and you realize that your son has failed to walk the dog after school and there is a puddle of dog urine on the living room rug, your temper flares and you find yourself yelling at your son in a manner that is probably an overreaction to the actual event.

The frustrating moments of your day were the slow triggers for your particular outburst. Small children also have similar slow triggers.

(Psst . . . The factors that make up the Whole Child, discussed in Chapter 3, if not addressed properly, will serve as slow triggers.)

Some examples of slow triggers:

Not enough sleep/fatigue	No advance warning prior to a change in activity
Hunger	Overstimulation
Lack of stimulation/boredom	The presentation of a task that is developmentally inappropriate
Chronic noise	Not enough praise/reinforcement for positive behavior
A change in routine	Unclear expectations
Illness	Not enough attention

As parents, we can oftentimes clearly recognize when our child is having an "off" day—a day that is more likely to contain an outburst. You know that she was put to bed too late because Grandma was visiting. You just got back from vacation and her routine has been disturbed. She didn't eat any breakfast. You had to rush her this morning because of a doctor's appointment. You're so preoccupied with unexpected work demands that you've relied too much on the television to babysit her. These factors can contribute to a child who is cranky and moody, and as a result, the child is at an increased risk of engaging in a temper outburst.

The parents' role: Sometimes parents can prevent or alleviate these slow triggers, making an outburst less likely to occur. But life isn't always predictable and slow triggers are going to occur.

Fast Triggers

A fast trigger is an event that immediately precedes a temper outburst. It is frequently assumed to be the direct cause of the outburst, but often multiple slow triggers have also contributed to the outburst. Fast triggers are events that cause a sudden spike in emotion, leading to the degeneration of coping skills and frustration tolerance.

For example, a fast trigger for a parent may include a child running near the road, just missing hitting a parked car while trying to park at the grocery store, a toddler striking an adult when angered, a computer unexpectedly shutting down, a spouse raising their voice, etc. All of these events cause a sudden emotional reaction that may elicit a quick emotional response.

> Take a few moments and write down some factors that work as "slow triggers" and "fast triggers" for your child. In addition, write these down for yourself. Oftentimes, a child's outburst can be triggered by the emotional upset of a parent. Parents inadvertently role-model poor coping strategies all the time.

There are unlimited examples of fast triggers for children, but here are a few of the most common:

Peer aggression/getting hit or pushed	Feeling frightened
Item being taken away	Lack of attention/feeling ignored
Perceived unfairness	Physical pain/discomfort
Immediate physical need not met	Sudden loud noise
Removal of pleasurable activity	Getting hurt (emotionally or physically)

Slow triggers may play a significant role in the onset of the outburst, but it's the fast trigger that transforms a "bad mood" into a temper outburst. Behavior that was initially cranky, whining, or mildly aggressive may erupt into a comprehensive, kicking-and-screaming outburst once a fast trigger is introduced. Any ability to cope with slow triggers may be abandoned if confronted with a fast trigger.

The Parent's Role in Recognizing Triggers

The primary methods parents can use to predict both fast and slow triggers are: 1) awareness when the characteristics of the Whole Child (discussed in Chapter 3) aren't being properly accommodated and 2) observation of your child and the nature of his interaction with the environment and people surrounding him. If you know that your child's routine has been disrupted or his sensory needs aren't being addressed, then it stands to reason that your child's coping strategies may become compromised. As a result, he may experience emotional upheaval. Similarly, if you observe signs of emotional upset in your child (agitation, tearfulness, fatigue, or aggression), then realize that a sudden, less predictable fast trigger (for example, getting hit by a peer) is likely to have a significant impact on your child's ability to remain calm. In these circumstances, it may be helpful either to 1) address the needs of the Whole Child or 2) remove your child from a situation that is extremely likely to result in a temper outburst.

The Last Chance to Prevent It Part

After a trigger has occurred, there is occasionally a brief opportunity to prevent a temper outburst. Oftentimes, parents do this through the use of appeasement. We give in, lowering our expectations and turning a "no" into a "yes" without any reason other than a desire to avoid a power struggle or a confrontation with an angry toddler or preschooler.

> The Parent's Role: *Don't* appease. *Don't* lower your behavioral expectations. *Do* consider distracting, redirecting, assisting, or validating feelings.

Outbursts can be avoided, but appeasement is not the preferred method. The key is to maintain high behavioral expectations for your child, but use simple strategies to halt the negative emotions that are beginning to surge.

The Parent's Role: Simple Strategies to Avoid a Temper Outburst

1. Distraction

This strategy is most effective for younger children (ages one to three years). This consists of refocusing their attention to another object or activity in order to distract them from the negative experience at hand. Some examples may include:

- "Look! The garbage truck is here! Let's go watch the workers as they dump every-one's garbage into the noisy truck!"

- "Here, have a snack while we're waiting for your sister to finish her gymnastics class."

- "I know you're tired of waiting for your sister's soccer game to be over. Did you see that Ben is here too? I'll bet he'd like someone to kick the soccer ball with!"

2. Redirection/Deferment

This strategy consists of giving your child a directive in order to postpone the current activity until he can calm down enough to work on it productively, or change the expectation to another, equally preferred activity. Some examples may include:

- "Listen, set down your video game for now because I can see you're getting really frustrated. Grab your iPod® and choose a song for us to listen to while I'm making lunch."

- "Ugh, this science worksheet is hard. Let's take a break and work on math for a little while."

- "Let your brother play with his blocks by himself for a bit. In 10 minutes, you can ask him again if you can help."

3. Assistance

This strategy consists of identifying when your child's coping strategies are disintegrating and offering her some guidance so that her frustration level doesn't progress from mild to outburst-worthy. During these situations, you're taking advantage of the opportunity to provide direct instruction of a specific skill before she's lost control of her emotions. You also have the opportunity to coach her through the use of a coping strategy as you see her frustration mounting. Parents have to be mindful not simply to take over an activity, as this can interfere with a child's ability to develop self-control and independence. Some examples may include:

- You notice that your child is struggling to tie his shoes because he's anxious to go out and play with the friends who have just knocked on the door. You can 1) encourage him to slow down, assuring him that his friends will still be outside when he's finished or 2) encourage him to carefully tie one shoe while you assist with the other. After he successfully ties his shoes, you can praise his patience.

- Your child is playing a game with a peer. You hear them beginning to argue over the rules, their voices rising. You briefly soothe them, guide them through a discussion about compromising on the rules, and leave them to play.

- Your child is working on math homework. She becomes frustrated and near tears, vowing to give up on the assignment. You encourage her to take some deep breaths and take a break. Once she's calm, you help her work through the first problem, then leave her to solve the rest.

In the above scenarios, the goal isn't simply to "take over" or complete the task for the child. It's to reassure, encourage, or guide the child so he doesn't resort to engaging in a temper outburst. The goal should be to simply offer a minimum of support so that your child can rein in his negative emotions but still feel a sense of pride from accomplishing something challenging.

4. Validating feelings

This strategy consists of identifying and acknowledging your child's emotion in hopes of reducing her frustration level. Sometimes, you can reduce her negative feelings simply by acknowledging the feelings' existence. Validating feelings can alter the trajectory of an outburst from an out-of-control expression of anger and frustration to a small bout of tears, which is much easier for a parent to deal with. This strategy is even more effective if accompanied by a soothing gesture of physical affection, such as rubbing her back, hugging, or stroking her hair. Some examples of this strategy include:

> Your child cannot learn to moderate his emotions if he's never given the opportunity to express them. A temper outburst is just an uninhibited expression of emotion.

- "Sweetheart, I see that you are so disappointed about not being able to go to pre-school today. It's hard to wait another day to do something fun."
- "I see you're very angry that Patrick pushed you into the sandbox a minute ago. Come here and let me brush off that sand. It's hard when someone isn't being a good friend, isn't it?"
- "Trying to tie your shoes is so frustrating! It's hard to get your hands to move the right way, isn't it? Come here and let me see what you've done so far. I think you've got a good start."

The Ugly Part

This is the part of the outburst that parents tend to recount when they're regaling new parents with stories from the trenches:

"And then, she threw herself on the floor and screamed as though I was killing her. My mother-in-law was horrified and told me I should spank her immediately. We were in public! What was I supposed to do?"

Or:

"I told him he couldn't walk around the restaurant and bother the other diners, and he dumped his plate of food on the floor, started crying, and crawled under the table. When I told him to come out immediately, he wrapped his arms around the table leg and told me to 'shut up.' My husband ended up dragging him out while I held the table to keep it from tipping over. It was awful. We never went back to that restaurant."

This is the portion of the outburst that consists of a complete loss of control over the child's behavior and emotions. During this portion of the outburst, children are often irrational, act panicked, or become physically aggressive.

The Parent's Role During the Ugly Part

A parent's first priority while their child is having an outburst is to make sure the child remains physically safe. For example, the child should not be permitted to have a temper outburst in the middle of a parking lot or while sitting in a chair that is likely to tip backward.

While you must intervene enough during the ugly part of the outburst to make sure your child is safe, understand that you're not intervening in hopes of ending the outburst. Most parents want to end this portion of the outburst as quickly as possible, as they either feel embarrassed (especially if in public), angry (because their child is so loud, disobedient, and/or aggressive), or guilty (because they said "no," presumably). It is difficult to watch a child in the midst of an outburst due to the extent of their emotional arousal.

But this is the portion of the outburst that needs to be ignored.

There should be a complete absence of attention. Any attention during this time is akin to *encouraging* a child to have a temper outburst.

During the ugly part, it may be helpful to remember these four principles:

1. Your child must not be reinforced for this behavior.

Any time we give someone attention, we're reinforcing their behavior. So, try not to intervene during this portion of the outburst, even if it is to administer a consequence such as a time-out or scolding. Any attention at all is likely to increase the likelihood that the outburst will reoccur. Therefore, parents must resist the urge to interact with their child.

2. Your child is behaving inappropriately, regardless of how justified his emotions are.

Temper outbursts are often the result of very real, justifiable emotions. However, we have a responsibility as a parent to teach children how to deal with these emotions. Permitting them to scream, hit, kick, spit, or destroy property is not doing them any favors. Once parents acknowledge the inappropriateness of their child's behavior and recognize their role in reducing the likelihood of outbursts, ignoring this portion of the outburst may be easier.

3. Your child cannot be reasoned with right now.

As noted above, parents have a responsibility to teach their child how to deal with strong emotions. However, this portion of the outburst is not the time to do it. The child is completely unavailable for learning at this point.

4. Your child will eventually calm down.

Occasionally, I work with kids who have a propensity to "rage" for hours at a time. These situations are rare, and are typically the result of a long history of reinforcing temper outbursts, or possibly, the complications related to a diagnosis of a disorder associated with behavioral challenges—Autism, some genetic disorders, or mental illness. Most children's rages will last between two and twenty minutes if they are not reinforced with attention. All children will calm down if given enough time.

Soothing Techniques for Parents during the Ugly Part

It is during this portion of the outburst that a parent is most likely to lose his/her temper. After all, your child is screaming, demonstrating physical aggression, or saying hurtful things. Remember, your child is upset, and he's seeking a response from you. And most children would rather be the recipient of a negative response than no response at all.

In order to cope with this portion of the outburst, it's essential that the parent develop some self-soothing strategies. Temper outbursts are stressful for all involved. Although all children have temper outbursts, understanding this doesn't make them any less upsetting.

Therefore, if you examine the diagram labeled "The Anatomy of a Tantrum: The Parent" on page 116, you'll find that "Self-Soothing" on the parent diagram corresponds with "The Ugly Part" on the child diagram. In order for the child to "benefit" from an outburst, the parent has to remain calm enough to mindfully parent their way through the outburst. If the parent's emotions become just as heightened as the child's, the parent is going to be unable to coach the child through the outburst and use this as an opportunity to teach problem-solving and coping skills.

Sitting outside your child's bedroom and trying to identify which toy she's throwing against the door is counterproductive and is likely to lead to your own temper boiling over. I assure you, parent temper outbursts are even more unbecoming than those exhibited by young children. Therefore, the parent needs to develop their own self-soothing strategies. Remember, during the ugly part, your primary role is to ignore the child and allow her to express her emotions, as she's unavailable for learning at this point. Some simple examples of parent-focused soothing strategies may include:

1. Removing yourself from the near vicinity in order to minimize the noise factor

2. Engaging in a pleasurable activity, like sipping coffee, surfing the web, or watching a television show to distract you from the outburst

3. Doing something physical, such as scrubbing out the sink, doing stretches, or engaging in some light exercise to help alleviate your tension.

4. Breathing!

Tip: Try to avoid participating in pleasurable activities within eyesight of your outbursting child. He does not want to see you enjoying yourself (or *trying* to enjoy yourself) while he's so upset. You're not using soothing strategies to give the impression that you're uncompassionate to their angst; you're simply doing it so you can remain calm and in control of your own emotions.

The Turning Point

This is the portion of the outburst where the tide begins to turn. The child begins the transformation from a completely irrational beast into a slightly less inconsolable monster-child.

The parent's role during this portion of the outburst is to continue to ignore.

But be warned. During the "turning point" stage of the outburst, the child may revert back to the full-fledged irrational beast several times before she completely calms down. Some signs that a child is experiencing the "turning point" in the outburst may include:

- A slight reduction in noise (quieter screaming or crying)
- Less physical aggression
- Pauses between sobs or verbal statements
- Increased use of words that are rational and less mean-spirited (fewer verbal threats or insults, more words implying remorse or the need for sympathy or reassurance)

The Parent's Role During the Turning Point

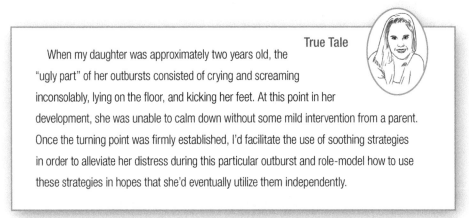

True Tale

When my daughter was approximately two years old, the "ugly part" of her outbursts consisted of crying and screaming inconsolably, lying on the floor, and kicking her feet. At this point in her development, she was unable to calm down without some mild intervention from a parent. Once the turning point was firmly established, I'd facilitate the use of soothing strategies in order to alleviate her distress during this particular outburst and role-model how to use these strategies in hopes that she'd eventually utilize them independently.

The Soothing/Self-soothing Part

This portion of the outburst begins once "the turning point" part of the outburst clearly indicates that the child is showing minor to moderate signs of calming down.

It is at this point that the parent must evaluate whether the child has the ability to use self-soothing strategies to calm down completely.

Small children require the use of simple soothing strategies that can be demonstrated and practiced over and over.

The Parent's Role in Helping Soothe Their Child

The ultimate goal for parents is to help their child learn how to soothe himself. Once this is accomplished, the child will presumably initiate the soothing strategies whenever their emotions escalate and avoid engaging in temper outbursts in the future. Some simple soothing strategies that can be conducted with children include:

1. Deep, slow breaths

This strategy consists of coaching your child through a series of deep, slow breaths. Encourage him to inhale through his nose and exhale through his mouth. Role-model this as you're explaining it to him. Continue to role-model it to him even if he refuses to do it. Praise him if he makes any effort to mimic you. You can further reinforce this strategy if you role-model this behavior for your children when you're feeling stressed or angry.

2. Slow counting

This strategy consists of coaching your child through the process of counting from one to ten in a slow, measured manner. The child can also be prompted to count backward as that may involve more mental effort, thereby distracting him from his negative thoughts. Once again, continue to role-model it to him even if he doesn't participate. Praise him if he makes any effort to mimic you.

3. Rubbing

• *Parent-facilitated:* As your child begins to calm down, rub his back, arms, or gently along his face to further soothe him. Encourage him to close his eyes.

• *Child-facilitated:* Encourage your child to soothe himself by closing his eyes and running his hands over his forehead, the sides of his face, and his arms.

These strategies will most likely have to be role-modeled dozens of times (or more!) before your child starts using them automatically.

If your child is older and/or has consistently demonstrated the ability to use self-soothing strategies to calm down (even if it's just that he cries until he's tired and then stops), then give him the space to do so. Don't interfere, as self-soothing is something that everyone benefits from learning, even into adulthood.

The Learning Opportunity/Teaching Moment

This portion of the outburst can only occur after the child is at least 80 to 90 percent calm. Hopefully, the child has been soothed enough to be receptive to dialogue, but is not so calm that he is impatient to move on to the next activity.

It is this portion of the tantrum that is typically underutilized by parents. Oftentimes, once parents see that their child has calmed, they'll encourage him to return to the original environment without further discussion. This completely overlooks the opportunity to teach a child an alternate behavior, because this is likely the first time since the outburst began that the child is available to learn something from his misbehavior. Parents should take advantage of their child's calm, attentive state to teach a replacement behavior—a behavior that meets the child's needs but is more socially appropriate.

The Parent's Role in the Teaching Moment

It is at this point that you refer back to the original trigger (most likely the fast trigger will appear most relevant) and discuss some alternative problem-solving strategies that could have been used to address the child's concern or emotional distress.

You may focus on:

1. What your child could have done to deal with the problem at hand

For example, maybe your four-year-old son had a temper outburst because a peer threw sand on him in the sandbox. As a result of the incident, he hit his peer, threw sand back, and screamed. During the teaching moment portion of the outburst, you may discuss with him the following: 1) finding someone else to play with if he sees that his peer is struggling to play nicely, 2) approaching an adult and asking for help in dealing with the situation, or 3) telling his peer in a firm but respectful manner to stop throwing sand and play nicely. During this portion of the outburst, you may also encourage your child to choose which of these possible solutions he prefers and then role-play how to do it accurately.

2. What your child could have done to deal with his negative emotions

Sometimes, the trigger of the outburst cannot be changed. In the above example, the child had an outburst because a peer threw sand on him in the sandbox. Therefore, during this learning opportunity, his mother may suggest that he walk away from such an anger-inducing situation in order to prevent him from getting more sand thrown on him and to calm himself so he doesn't behave in a manner that will get him in trouble. This teaching moment may also consist of practicing the coping strategies used during the "soothing" portion of the outburst, talking about which words can be best used to identify and describe feelings, discussing how to identify the physical signs of an imminent outburst ("How do you feel right before you start crying? Do you feel sweaty? Do you feel like you're taking fast breaths?") or brainstorming more acceptable ways to show strong emotion (talking it out, taking some time alone in your room, drawing an angry picture, etc.).

> It's important to acknowledge that the outburst has come to an end so that the child doesn't associate any positive attention and activities that occur after the outburst as being related to the outburst in any way, as this could inadvertently reinforce the outburst.

The Kiss and Make Up Part

Once the outburst is clearly over, it's time to move on without looking back. This means that the outburst should not be mentioned repeatedly, nor should the ugly part be referred to again. As the teaching moment portion of the outburst draws to a close, it's time to give your child a verbal cue to indicate that the time spent on this particular interaction has been discontinued and that you're moving onto the next activity. By putting closure on the tantrum and proceeding to the next portion of their day, you're role-modeling forgiveness and demonstrating confidence that they'll make better choices in the future.

The Parent's Role in the Making Up Part

Mom: Luke, I think you're feeling better now. I like how calm you are, and I appreciate you trying to count to ten with me. Let's be all done here and go find something else to do. Can I give you a kiss and a hug?

One way to cue the end of the interaction is to ask for a kiss or a hug. Hug tightly, say sweet things, and find a new activity. This is a method that can be used well into adulthood to show forgiveness, demonstrate a loving attitude, and move past a negative interaction.

In my house after a temper outburst, my son would ask, "Is it time for the kissing and hugging part, Mommy?" Older children may prefer a high-five, a fist-bump, or a simple statement acknowledging the outburst's conclusion and the progression to the next activity. Regardless of how it's communicated, the end of the outburst should be acknowledged.

Question: What about the Children Who Can "Turn Off" an Outburst Extremely Quickly?

Cara, age three, is attempting to earn an Olympic medal in temper outbursts. Her mother reports that she has an excessive amount of outbursts, often over small events like not getting to use the pink plastic cup or not getting to the sink before her sister to wash her hands. Her mother has noticed that even if Cara appears to be in the midst of a terrible outburst characterized by tears, screaming, and hitting (the ugly part), she stops immediately if her original request is granted. Her mom wants to know if what Cara is experiencing is really a temper outburst.

Answer: Yes, it is. It's just that she's learned to *exhibit the signs* of emotional distress prior to *actually* experiencing emotional distress, as she's discovered that once the signs of emotional distress are presented, she is likely to be appeased. It's probable that true emotional distress would prevail if appeasement was taken away as a viable response to her outburst. In this situation, the parent may be able to use the strategies described in "the last chance to prevent it" portion to ward off the outburst. Additionally, as noted in Chapter 6, parents should prioritize the behavioral expectations that they perceive to be the most important and avoid engaging in a power struggle unnecessarily.

Don't be Frightened of Temper Outbursts

It's no secret—parents hate temper outbursts. Outbursts can be noisy, embarrassing, and anger-provoking for parents if they don't learn to deal with their own emotions during them. Once a parent has mastered the ability not to take their child's outbursts personally and understand them to be an inappropriate mode of emotional expression, outbursts are dreaded less. This results in parents who don't attempt to avoid outbursts by using appeasement or lowering their behavioral expectations.

Children will not suffer long-term emotional maladjustment from a temper outburst, particularly if it's not overreacted to and they're kept physically safe. And as most parents can attest, temper outbursts often occur for relatively minor reasons, such as from the refusal of a request or having a toy snatched out of a child's hands by a peer. Outbursts will occur more frequently and be exhibited at an older age if they're not addressed in a healthy way. Children need the chance to have outbursts, learn that they're an ineffective way to get what they want, and move on to more mature techniques of getting their needs met.

Children should learn that while all feelings are okay, all emotional expression is not. From an early age, children should be taught (and role-modeled) how to convey emotion so that it's done in a healthy, empowered way. Hitting, screaming, throwing things, and otherwise losing control are likely to result in guilt, a sense of failure, and impaired relationships if they extend past a young age. There have been many times when my five-year-old has marveled, "Why is he screaming like that, Mommy?" when a peer engages in a temper outburst for what appears to be a minor reason. My son is aware that this behavior is inappropriate and atypical for his age group.

As a parent, my desire is to teach my children how to manage their emotions at a young age so they develop healthy patterns that will last well into adulthood. The primary methods to teach healthy coping strategies are first to role-model them and next to provide direct instruction via clear and direct descriptions, role-playing when the child is calm, and guiding the child through using the strategies when the child is upset. Finally, parents should remember to reinforce their child via praise or physical affection (*"Katie, I saw you take a deep breath when Charlie grabbed that toy from you. That was fantastic."*) when the child demonstrates a healthy coping strategy.

Key Points Discussed in Chapter 7

- Traditional temper outbursts can be defined by a complete loss of emotional control by the child. They are most likely to occur between the ages of one and four years. Temper outbursts are a typical part of child development.

- Children have temper outbursts for various reasons: they don't have the language skills to communicate their wants and needs appropriately, they have poorly developed frustration tolerance or impulse control, they may be searching for autonomy or a sense of control over their environment, or they've learned that it's a successful strategy to get what they want.

- There are seven stages of a temper outburst: the trigger, the last chance to prevent it part, the ugly part, the turning point, the self-soothing/soothing part, the learning opportunity/teaching moment, and the kiss and make up part.

- Increasing your awareness, as the parent, of how you are reacting emotionally to the outburst can help control your behavioral reaction to the outburst.

- Distraction, redirection/deferment, assistance, or validating feelings are all strategies parents can use to prevent a temper outburst.

- Simple soothing strategies include deep, slow breaths; slow counting; and rubbing. The parent will initially facilitate these strategies with the hope that the child will eventually use them independently.

- Temper outbursts are necessary, as they are a precursor to developing more appropriate long-term coping strategies.

Notes:

Chapter 8

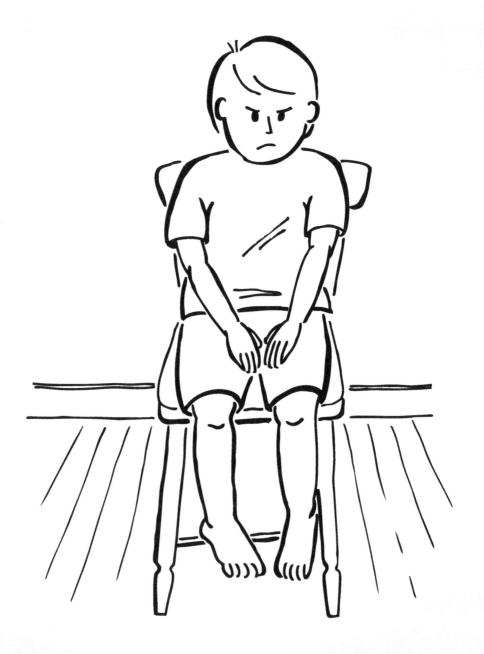

How to Use Punishment Effectively

In an ideal world, children would learn to develop pro-social behavior solely through the use of positive reinforcement. We'd simply attend to our child's desirable behavior and lavish him or her with praise to encourage its repetition. Misbehavior, if it occurred at all, would simply be ignored so as not to reinforce it via attention.

Despite the effectiveness of positive reinforcement, however, its use cannot guarantee that a child will consistently demonstrate appropriate behavior. At times, parents must use punishment in conjunction with reinforcement in order to maximize likelihood that misbehavior will be extinguished and positive behavior will reoccur. Punishment is a term that has negative connotations because people tend to associate this term with harsh methods of discipline such as yelling or spanking. In reality, punishment is simply the process of adding something unpleasant to the environment *or* taking away something desirable after misbehavior occurs to *decrease* the likelihood of misbehavior.

The diagram below revisits the concepts introduced in Chapter 2, reminding us that once a behavior is exhibited, there is a reaction within the environment. Depending on this reaction, the behavior can be *reinforced* (encouraged or rewarded) or *punished* (strongly discouraged). If the behavior is reinforced, it is much more likely to be repeated.

Although reinforcement has been discussed extensively in Chapter 4, it's important to contrast it with punishment, as punishment is a behavioral management strategy that is often misused.

Punishment can take two forms: 1) adding something aversive after misbehavior occurs, such as scolding or time-out; or 2) taking away something desirable after misbehavior occurs, such as the removal of privileges (e.g., the use of a cell phone or time with friends) or an item (e.g., dessert). The type of punishment used depends on the child and the nature of his or her misbehavior. As noted in Chapter 6, punishments that evolve from natural and logical consequences are preferred, as they are most likely to lead to intrinsically motivated behavior.

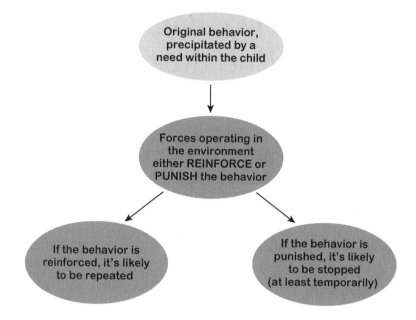

Effects on Behavior of Reinforcement and Punishment

Before punishment is incorporated into your repertoire of behavioral management strategies, however, consider the following components of effective punishment.

Five Necessary Components for Effective Punishment

1. *The punishment should be applied immediately following the misbehavior.*

If a child misbehaves in the grocery store, the punishment is going to lose effectiveness if it's distributed after a significant time lapse. This is especially true for younger children. Imagine a child who spends an entire visit to the grocery store having a temper outburst because she isn't permitted to choose some cookies to purchase. Instead of giving a time-out immediately, Dad waits until they arrive home one hour later and directs his daughter to sit on a dining room chair for four minutes due to her excessive crying in the store.

This would be ineffective because 1) the child has calmed down and has likely forgotten about the event, and 2) she is unlikely to understand the direct cause and effect relationship between misbehavior and punishment. Therefore, the punishment is ineffective. And because, from her perspective, her misbehavior has remained unpunished, she is more likely to engage in the misbehavior at a future visit to the grocery store.

2. The punishment should be applied consistently—each time the misbehavior occurs.

In order for a child to receive a strong message that a particular behavior is unacceptable, the punishment must be distributed each time the misbehavior occurs. Otherwise, the child receives the message that sometimes the behavior is tolerated. If the misbehavior is particularly fun (jumping on all the furniture in the furniture store in your quest to purchase a new couch), the reward of engaging in the behavior will far surpass the unpleasant nature of a punishment distributed sporadically. And each time the misbehavior goes unpunished, you are sending your child the message that the misbehavior is acceptable.

3. Punishment should be used to teach, not to demonstrate spite or revenge.

There is one purpose of punishment: to send a firm but compassionate message to a child that a particular misbehavior is unacceptable. Punishment should not be used with the intent to impart unnecessary discomfort or emotional distress. As stated in Chapter 7, parents often have a significant emotional response to misbehavior and may benefit from the use of self-soothing strategies before imparting a punishment.

4. Punishment should be followed with direct instruction toward the acceptable behavior.

Imagine you are starting a new job. On your first day, you are instructed to "do a good job," and little instruction or training is provided. Naturally, you flail about, attempting various tasks in hopes that you are completing them successfully.

Now, imagine that each time you complete a task unsuccessfully, your pay is reduced by ten dollars per day. Will docking your pay make you more competent at your job? Will you become magically educated on the "correct" way to complete your new responsibilities? Or will it simply result in discouragement and a sense of failure? In order to learn from your mistakes, you need direction about what you *should* be doing. (Actually, it would have been best if you'd been provided with appropriate instruction *prior* to attempting your new job, as *avoiding* mistakes would be the most rewarding.)

5. The severity of the punishment should correspond to the severity of the misbehavior.

In order for a child to truly absorb the message that you are trying to send her about a particular misbehavior, the punishment needs to be appropriate in its severity and distributed fairly. A poor grade on a spelling test should not result in the loss of privileges for one month. This is an overreaction and reduces the effectiveness of a punishment, as the child will focus more on your punitive nature than on remediating her poor studying habits.

Pitfalls to Punishment

1. *Punishment is reactive, rather than proactive. In contrast, reinforcement can be used to prevent misbehavior from ever occurring.* In other words, punishment only serves to tell children what *not* to do, as it's administered after misbehavior has already occurred. Alternatively, reinforcement can be administered whenever a positive behavior is observed in order to teach children what they *should* do. Because the focus should be on rewarding the positive behavior, reinforcement

   > The best way to deal with misbehavior is to prevent it.

   should be the sole strategy used to address misbehavior whenever possible.

   Tip: Don't punish your child before the misbehavior occurs. Can you imagine? "Son, I'm taking away your cell phone in anticipation of you acting like a hoodlum in church on Sunday." No. We may give *advance warning* of punishment—"If you hit any of your friends while we're at the park, then we're going home immediately"—but we shouldn't actually administer punishment until misbehavior occurs.

2. *Punishment is a term that is oftentimes viewed unfavorably by the general public (and parents in particular).* Because of this, parents are reluctant to use it. If they aren't invested in using it and/or they don't know how, it is unlikely to be used effectively. After all, who wants to brag about how their child is so well behaved because the parent is able to use punishment appropriately?

   Innocent bystander: "My goodness, your children are so well behaved! I'm so impressed. How is it that you've taught them to be such good listeners?"

   You: "Oh, I'm great at using punishment effectively."

Reinforcement and Punishment

3. ***Positive behavior is more likely to become intrinsically motivated when good behavior is reinforced than when misbehavior is punished.*** Punishment, because of its inherent inability to teach positive behavior, tends to be effective only because children gravitate *away* from misbehavior in order to *avoid* the punishment. Whenever a child is motivated to do something, especially if it's intrinsically motivated, it more quickly becomes part of their habitual pattern of behavior and is more likely to be repeated in the future.

Time-out

Time-out is typically one of the primary methods of discipline that parents gravitate toward, as it seems to be straightforward in its approach, is often recommended by pediatricians and therapists, can be used in many settings, and can be used by both parents and child care professionals.

What is Time-out?

Time-out is the temporary, quiet removal of a child from the environment in which he or she misbehaved. Its intent is to simply eliminate reinforcement from the child's environment. It has the benefit of separating the parent's emotions from the misbehavior, minimizing the likelihood that the parent will lose their temper.

The Four Myths of Time-out

Myth #1: Time-out is an "easy" consequence to administer. You simply tell the child to sit in the corner for a few minutes.

Truth: There is a "right" and a "wrong" way to use time-out. It should be administered with forethought and mindfulness, rather than impulse and impatience. Not understanding its purpose, the reasons for which it should be used, or how to implement it so that its effectiveness is maximized is sabotaging the likelihood of its success in decreasing misbehavior and increasing positive behavior.

Myth #2: Time-out is "mean" to use with toddlers because they don't understand what is happening.

Truth: If used correctly, time-out is a safe and gentle way to provide consequences for toddlers who misbehave. Ideally, time-out is a strategy that should be initiated while the child is young (18 months), as it is a process with a specific purpose that needs to be taught.

Myth #3: Time-out is used to teach children how to behave.

Truth: Time-out is a form of punishment, as it is the process of adding something aversive to decrease misbehavior. Because it is an effective punishment with minimal physical or emotional side effects, it is a preferred punishment. However, simply punishing a child for misbehavior does not necessarily result in a child exhibiting an appropriate behavior. While it may discourage a particular misbehavior, the only way an appropriate behavior will be acquired is to teach it. This requires more than simply issuing a time-out.

Myth #4: If time-out doesn't appear to "work" right away (by decreasing the misbehavior), it's probably because it's not a good approach for your particular child.

Truth: Once time-out is introduced as a method of discipline, the misbehavior often initially increases in frequency and intensity. As you place a boundary around a child's behavior, she will initially respond by pushing back harder than ever. This is because she's probably had experience with you "caving" when she misbehaves, so she's going to try to get you to revert to that default behavior. Over time, your adherence to effective time-out strategies will send a clear, consistent message that the misbehavior will no longer be reinforced. Therefore, the misbehavior will decrease in intensity and frequency, hopefully becoming completely extinguished.

Let's look at an example:

Leo, a three-year-old boy, has a fourteen-month-old sister, Lucy. Leo's mother frequently reprimands Leo for playing too aggressively with Lucy, as he often takes her toys, causes her to fall over, or yells into her face when she touches his things. When Leo gets too aggressive, his mom typically reminds him several times to "be nice to Lucy," and when he doesn't listen, she joins the pair and plays with them, providing Leo with excessive attention so that he'll not be as likely to prey on his sister.

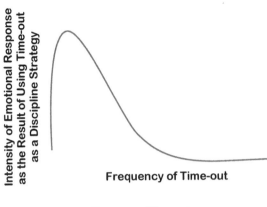

Frequency of Time-out

Frequency of Time-out

*Eventually, Leo's mom recognizes that her attention is simply reinforcing Leo's aggression toward Lucy, so she decides to start implementing time-out with Leo. The first time she tells him to go to time-out for playing aggressively with Lucy, he goes relatively complacently and is pleased when his mom praises him for following directions. The second time, he becomes enraged at being told to leave the social environment and begins throwing toys and shrieking, "I hate you!" It takes nearly 15 minutes for him to calm down. During the next 10 occasions that time-out is used, Leo's outbursts continue to be loud and rather lengthy, as he hates being "ignored" in time-*out *and is hoping his dramatic emotional response will elicit sympathy from his mother. It's only after experiencing time-out repeatedly and consistently that he realizes that his outbursts*

Losing your temper is simply a sign that you've waited too long to administer reasonable consequences. Losing your temper also increases the likelihood that you will administer time-out in a less mindful way, possibly reducing its effectiveness.

are futile—misbehavior will result in a time-out regardless of his emotional outburst. In fact, his emotional outburst only serves to extend the length of time-out.

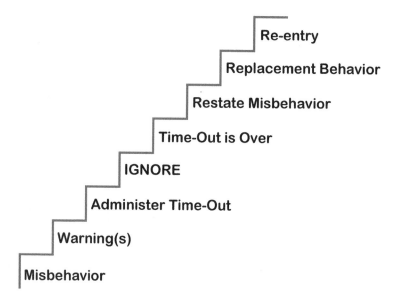

Stages of a Time-out

Seven Steps for an Effective Time-out

Obviously, a parent only administers time-out after observing misbehavior. However, keep in mind that first you need to:

a. Clearly identify the misbehavior.

When you refer to the misbehavior, use clear, specific terms that clearly describe the behavior. Simply saying "Stop being annoying" or "Behave" are less effective directives than "Please lower your voice; you're talking too loudly" or "Please stop banging your toys on the table."

b. Suggest another, more acceptable behavior.

Suggest an acceptable behavior that your child should do instead of the misbehavior. This may consist of a directive such as "I'd like you to say 'please' instead of grabbing" or "I'd like you to put that away and wash your hands."

c. State the consequences for continuing to misbehave.

By warning the child that a time-out is imminent if a more positive behavior isn't displayed, you're actually presenting the child with a choice—she can continue the misbehavior and be sent to a time-out, or she can engage in a more acceptable behavior and avoid a time-out.

Once it's been determined that a time-out is appropriate, the following steps are recommended:

Step 1: Provide at least one warning (but no more than two) to the child.

After you've identified the misbehavior, suggested a more acceptable behavior, and stated the consequences for continuing to misbehave, provide one or two warnings prior to placing your child in time-out.

Step 2: Place the child in time-out.

Direct your child to the time-out area. At this time, the misbehavior should be referred to with a few simple words in a matter-of-fact tone so that the child has a clear understanding of exactly why he is being sent there. Providing a lengthy explanation is likely to be counterproductive, as 1) you've already given them at least one warning, and 2) if he were in the mood to listen and learn from your wise explanation, he probably wouldn't be misbehaving.

Two Things to Consider When Choosing a Time-out Spot:

1. Time-out just turns into a power struggle if you can't keep the child in the time-out spot.

One of the most common reasons why parents report that time-out doesn't work is because they can't find a way to keep their child in the time-out location. They indicate that they try time-out locations such as the couch, the bottom step of the stairway, a spot on the floor, a dining room chair, etc. These are all places where a child can easily leave the area, and when the child does so, a power struggle ensues between the parent and the child.

Remember, time-out is defined as "the temporary, quiet removal of a child from the environment in which they misbehaved." However, it's hard to have the "removal" portion of the time-out if the child keeps leaving the time-out location.

Therefore, if you place the child in a time-out spot for the first time and she leaves and doesn't immediately return and remain when you redirect her in a firm voice, consider establishing a time-out location that doesn't permit the child to leave at will. Some recommendations for time-out areas include:

- A high-chair that's pulled away from the table and placed in another location
- A Pack 'n Play®
- A small, safe, boring room (such as a nearly empty laundry room) with the door open and a baby gate blocking the door

(Pssttt... Finding a time-out spot that can't be left at will is easier when the child is smaller. This is a compelling reason to begin using time-outs when the child is still relatively young.)

2. **Location, location, location.**

Another common error of parents who perceive time-out to be an unsuccessful punishment is conducting time-out in a busy or entertaining area in the house. Time-out should be somewhere totally boring and un-fun. It should be a place that is safe and within earshot of an adult (particularly if the child is very young), but somewhere isolated enough that no one is going to walk by and do something interesting. It should not be in the line of sight of the television, another person, or an interesting view outside the window. The child shouldn't be able to hear conversation, radio, or television, although it's fine if he "hears" his parent bustling around in the other room, knowing full well that they are not going to be paying attention to him at this time. Some suggested locations in the house may include:

- Against the wall in the dining room you never use
- In the hallway that no one will pass through
- In the corner of an empty, silent room

(Pssttt, again... When the child "learns" the time-out process and is well versed in the fact that time-out is nonnegotiable, he is unlikely to resist time-out. Eventually it can be done anywhere, even in public.)

Finally, be mindful that the location of the time-out doesn't result in a negative association with another desired behavior. For example, if the child is a poor eater, it may not be wise to conduct time-out in his high chair, even if the chair is moved to another room. If the child is a poor sleeper, it may not be advisable to place her in a Pack 'n Play® or her crib.

Step 3: Ignore, ignore, ignore.

This portion of the time-out is unequivocally the most important part. Recall that the definition of time-out is "the quiet, temporary removal of a child from the environment in which they misbehaved." However, it's hard to have the "quiet" portion if you spend the entire time-out making statements like "As soon as you stop crying, you can come out of time-out."

Some parents maintain a constant stream of chatter that consists of scolding, lecturing, cajoling, bribing, or distracting. But the purpose of time-out is to remove the child from the environment in which he misbehaved. Presumably, this environment is either 1) an appealing environment, upon which removal will be met with disappointment, or 2) an overwhelming environment, in which children will benefit from regrouping and hitting the "restart" button on their behavior. Regardless, most children dislike being deprived of attention and find time-out to be upsetting.

> Remember, attention is innately reinforcing. If you provide attention to a child during time-out, you're making time-out a positive experience. Time-out should be boring and un-fun, as it is punishment.

Therefore, it is crucial that this portion of time-out be completely silent and completely non-reinforcing. Remember, your child will only be in time-out for a few moments; as long as he's safe, ignoring him for this short period of time will not hurt him physically or emotionally.

Step 4: Time-out can be concluded only if the child isn't in hysterics, saying hateful things, or acting physically aggressive.

When children are very young (age two), appropriate time-out behaviors should be reinforced very quickly in the time-out process. For example, if you place a child in time-out for throwing a toy (after two warnings) and she sits in the time-out spot in a compliant manner, her time-out should be very brief with praise at its conclusion.

However, for older children who have experienced time-out on enough occasions to be familiar with the process, the length of time-out should fall approximately within the range of one minute per year of the child (five minutes = age five) or last until the child is relatively calm (whichever comes last). If the five minutes have passed and the child is still in the throes of a temper outburst (see Chapter 7), the temper outburst must be resolved before the time-out is concluded. Releasing a child from time-out while she is engaging in hysterics, saying hateful things, or being physically aggressive (shaking the side of the Pack 'n Play®, kicking the wall, etc.) simply reinforces the emotional outburst, making it more likely that it will occur at a later time. However, if she is in control but unhappy (crying sadly), the time-out can be concluded.

For example:

"Bethany, you did a great job staying in time-out like I asked. But you are not to hit. If you feel angry, you come to Mommy and say, 'Help me, Mommy,' and I will help you. Do not hit."

In this example, you are praising Bethany in order to reinforce appropriate time-out behavior: remaining in the time-out location.

Step 5: Restate the misbehavior.

As noted in the above sample about Bethany, the parent needs to remind the child of the misbehavior that resulted in the time-out. This is to reinforce the relationship between the misbehavior and the time-out, as children may have forgotten its purpose if they became overemotional during their sad and lonely moments in seclusion.

The reminder of the misbehavior should be brief, clear, and made in a matter-of-fact but firm voice.

Step 6: State the replacement behavior. Teach a more acceptable behavior. Reinforce the acceptable behavior.

As noted in Step 1, restating the misbehavior is not enough to guarantee that your child is going to make a better choice next time. Oftentimes, we focus on telling our child what not to do rather than what to do. Therefore, once the child is reminded of the misbehavior and its relationship to time-out, we need to transfer our attention to identifying, teaching, and reinforcing a more acceptable behavior. This new, positive behavior is known as the "replacement behavior."

Step 7: Return to the original environment.

Once time-out is concluded, the misbehavior is revisited, and a replacement behavior is identified, taught, and reinforced, it's time for the child to re-enter the original environment. Although occasional reminders or prompting may be needed to remind the child not to revert to the misbehavior (*"Remember, Joshua, if you need help, ask Mrs.*

Wendell in your big-boy voice, not a whiny voice. You did a great job earlier when we practiced"), there should not be an aura of "you naughty child, you just got in trouble" hanging over the remainder of the interaction. The child misbehaved, the consequence was administered, and now it's time to move on.

There should be a point of re-entry to the original environment and closure of the time-out process. A kiss or a hug is a good way to de-escalate the emotions in the room (as oftentimes the parent is very upset or frustrated at the time the child enters time-out). After the hug, give your child one last reminder of the replacement behavior, and encourage them to make better choices. If re-entry to the original environment simply consists of "Okay, time-out is done. You can go back out to play," and you don't capitalize on the teaching opportunity, your child is much more likely to be back in the time-out spot within a short period of time.

Time-out in a Public Place

Once time-out is mastered in the home setting, it can be generalized to a public setting. It may be helpful first to try it in other people's homes, such as when you're on a playdate or at a family member's house. The key component to a successful away-from-home time-out is not having the child leave the time-out area at will.

True Tale

When my daughter was five and my son was three, they were behaving rambunctiously in a home goods store. They were acting silly, misusing items on the shelves, and generally being disruptive. After giving two warnings, I told them to take a time-out and pointed to a bare spot on a bottom shelf. They each sat quietly for a couple minutes while I browsed the aisle. After three or four moments, I praised them for behaving appropriately during time-out, reminded them of my behavioral expectations, and gave them a replacement behavior. As we moved to another aisle, a woman approached me and asked how on earth I was able to make my children sit there so quietly without moving or crying. I simply told her that my children had extensive experience with time-out and knew that they needed to use their quiet time as a chance to regroup, or else the punishment would become more severe later (such as the withdrawal of our afternoon trip to a neighbor's house to play).

A "Self" Time-out

A "self" time-out is when the child has participated in the time-out process long enough to sense when she needs to take some quiet time to calm herself down or think about making better choices. Adults use this effective strategy all the time—we escape to the bathroom, shut the door to our office, or fold laundry in the laundry room to escape the chaos in the family room. Although we often role-model this strategy, it's important to consciously teach it to our children as it's an excellent lesson in self-control and decision making.

A self time-out is an optional time-out. It's a suggestion. A parent might say to their child, "Addison, I can see that your brother is frustrating you because he's playing the Wii very noisily. Do you need a break from him? I feel like you might be tempted to kick him from your spot on the couch, and I don't want you to get in trouble. What do you think?"

Sometimes parents will use this term openly: "Do you need a self time-out? Go take one; we have time before we leave." Other times, parents just encourage the child to examine his frustration level and take a quiet moment if he feels it would be helpful. This strategy can be introduced as early as age three or four, but is an essential tool to use with older children. Encouraging them to self-evaluate and tap into their coping skills can significantly de-escalate an emotional situation and establish a healthy pattern of "stopping and thinking" prior to getting into an argument or making a poor decision.

It should also be noted that this type of time-out is very helpful for children who struggle with sensory overload, as they benefit from removing themselves from an overstimulating environment.

Apologizing: Should We Force Our Child to Apologize?

We've all witnessed or been part of a situation where a parent compels their child to apologize to another child due to their misbehavior. It often goes something like this:

Mom: Wyatt, you need to apologize to Ryan for pushing him off of his scooter.

Wyatt: (stony silence)

Mom: Wyatt, you need to say you're sorry.

Ryan: (very uncomfortable)

Mom: Wyatt . . .

Wyatt (angrily): Sorry.

Mom: For what?

Wyatt: For pushing.

Mom: I'd like you to look at him while you say it.

Ryan: (squirming and wanting this interaction to be over)

Wyatt (briefly darts eyes at Ryan): Sorry.

Mom (gives up): Fine. Go play.

Being able to apologize with maturity and sincerity is a skill that will benefit an individual for a lifetime. It's a crucial life skill that is often overlooked. Yet so few children know how to do it well—primarily, I suspect, because so few adults know how to do it appropriately. So the question is: Should we "make" our children apologize when they've behaved in a matter that was unkind, selfish, or inconsiderate?

First, let's talk about some pros and cons of "making" our child apologize.

Pros of "Making" Your Child Apologize

1. It compels them to take responsibility for their behavior. An apology requires them to admit they were wrong.

2. It's a good social skill. It breeds forgiveness and goodwill in the person who was wronged and thus helps to maintain relationships.

3. Because apologizing is usually awkward and somewhat embarrassing, it's an extension of the punishment. Maybe the child will think twice before they do something unkind and are made to apologize again.

4. Children aren't going to learn to apologize independently if they have never been asked to practice it. What starts out as "making them" will surely transform to something more intrinsic, right?

Cons of "Making" Your Child Apologize

1. Because you (the adult) are making the child apologize, the child is likely to divorce himself from a sense of responsibility over his actions. His inner dialogue goes from "Wow, I did something unkind and I feel bad about it" to "Darn it, Mom. He started it. Why do I have to take the blame?" The child's resentment

about being forced to apologize detracts from his introspection about his own behavior.

2. It's not a good social skill if the apology is extended awkwardly or resentfully. In addition, the other person typically feels uncomfortable and embarrassed too, which brings further negativity to the social interaction.

3. Apologies are meaningless if they aren't genuine and the child is unable to understand the value of extending an apology to a person whom they've wronged.

4. Kids aren't going to learn to apologize independently if they've never been given the decision-making power to determine when and how they apologize.

I think there are some strong reasons for each side with regard to this issue. Personally, I don't "make" my kids apologize, but I discuss with them the following:

1. What they did wrong; why an apology is needed.

2. How I would prefer that they apologize, although it's ultimately their choice.

3. The benefits of apologizing (how they and the wronged person might feel better and will be able to move on).

4. How they can do it quickly and appropriately (using role play).

Ultimately, I feel the best way to teach a child to apologize is for the parents to role-model it; with each other, with their children, and with friends and extended family. It should be role-modeled in a sincere way, with the person who is apologizing doing the following:

1. Stating the person's name ("Leah, I'm really sorry . . .").

2. Referring back to the specific behavior for which they're sorry.

3. Indicating why this behavior was so hurtful or inconsiderate.

4. Identifying a replacement behavior.

"Leah, I'm really sorry for calling you 'stupid.' It was mean. Instead of getting so mad, I should have asked my mom to help."

"Tommy, I'm sorry for scribbling on your picture. I shouldn't have ruined it. Next time, I'll ask before I touch it."

"Addison, I'm sorry I pulled your hair. I know it hurt. I won't do it again."

Key Points Discussed in Chapter 8

- Punishment is the process of adding something unpleasant to the environment to decrease the likelihood of misbehavior. There are two types: adding something aversive after misbehavior occurs and taking away something desirable after misbehavior occurs.

- Punishment can be very effective if it 1) is applied immediately following the misbehavior, 2) is applied consistently, 3) isn't used spitefully, 4) is followed with direct instruction in the acceptable behavior, and 5) corresponds to the severity of the misbehavior.

- Although punishment can be effective, it should always be secondary to reinforcement. In contrast to punishment, reinforcement is proactive, is viewed positively by the general public, helps teach children how to behave, and is more likely to lead to behavior that is intrinsically motivated.

- Time-out is the temporary, quiet removal of a child from the environment in which they misbehaved.

- Ideally, time-out is a consequence that should be implemented as early as 18 months, as it requires several behaviors (remaining in time-out, self-soothing/calming down, and participating in a discussion about replacement behaviors) that need to be taught.

- Time-out in and of itself won't teach children how to behave; it's a punishment. However, the time immediately following the time-out can be allocated for discussing and teaching pro-social behavior.

- Initially, the use of time-out may result in an increase in the frequency and intensity of misbehavior. The child will rebel against it, hoping that you'll capitulate to their demands and outbursts, particularly during the "ignore" portion.

- Time-out isn't simply a matter of telling a child to sit in the corner. There are seven steps to follow to ensure an effective time-out practice:
  1. Prior to administering a time-out, provide at least one warning.
  2. Place the child in time-out. Choose a time-out spot that is secluded and boring.
  3. Ignore the child completely during the time-out (this is the most important step).
  4. Conclude time-out only if the child isn't in hysterics, saying hateful things, or being physically aggressive.
  5. Restate the misbehavior.
  6. State the replacement behavior. Teach a more acceptable behavior. Reinforce the acceptable behavior.
  7. Return to the original environment.

- A "self time-out" is a strategy that is less about punishment and more about coping and self-monitoring.

- There are pros and cons to "making" our child apologize. It is ultimately up to the parent to decide what is more compatible with their parenting style.

Chapter 9

The Parent Toolbox: Applying What We Know

We've talked about reinforcement. Nurturing communication. Listening behavior. Power struggles. Temper outbursts. Punishment. We've talked about how these principles, if used effectively and in conjunction with one another, contribute to better behavior. The interaction between you and your child can transition from frustrating and negative to respectful and positive.

By using the behavioral model referred to throughout this book, I am going to show you how to directly apply the tools and concepts from this book to real-life situations.

Transitions

Ask any parent or teacher, and you'll learn that a significant portion of misbehavior occurs during transitions from one activity to another. Regardless of the type of transition—from home to school or mealtime to bathtime—the act of changing gears from one activity to another (and all the steps that this entails) can result in misbehavior such as dawdling, poor listening, temper outbursts, refusal behavior, avoidance, and irritability.

Like any behavior, transitions need to be *learned*. Wander down the kindergarten hallway at any elementary school during the first week of school and you'll find teachers with

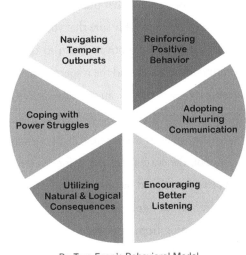

Dr. Tara Egan's Behavioral Model

their five- and six-year-old charges marching up and down the hallway, practicing transitions. They know that they can't tell young children, "We're going to lunch now," and expect it to proceed smoothly.

Therefore, in order to address skill deficits, you need to *teach* transitions. The most effective way is to role-play—act them out with your child. You'll probably feel very silly doing it. I, after eight years of parenting, still feel ridiculous role-playing social interactions, bedtime behavior, or appropriate behavior to be demonstrated while in public. But it works.

For example, each morning for a full week before school begins, practice your school morning routine. Have your children help you lay out their clothes the night before. Roust them at the appropriate hour in the morning. Proceed through each step—bathroom time, dressing/hair combing, breakfast, and tooth brushing. Give encouragement, explain, and use hand-over-hand assistance to teach skills (we had many mornings of hand-over-hand instruction in how to tuck a shirt into dress pants in order to adhere to the dress code at my children's public school). By the time the first day of school rolls around, all the kinks will have been ironed out and your morning will move along more smoothly. You'll know that if your child balks at getting ready for school, it's probably due to anxiety or not enough sleep (or *your* unpreparedness), not because he doesn't know what to do or how to do it.

And if you get off track, you can simply re-enact the role play and remind everyone involved how to make that transition.

Once you're reasonably sure that your child knows the steps to transition successfully, it's time to actually motivate them to transition nicely. This is where the nurturing communication style and the respect it elicits come into play. If your child is engaged in an activity—whether it's an enjoyable activity that will be hard to tear them away from (such as watching a favorite television show), or an activity that requires concentration and focus (such as attempting to tie a shoe), they deserve the chance to have some closure on the current activity before they're expected to transition to a new one. This can be accomplished by giving an *advance warning.*

There are two strategies for giving an advance warning for daily transitions, such as transitioning from playtime to bedtime. They are the *two-minute rule* and the *two-more-times rule.*

The *two-minute rule*, once firmly established, works very well with young children. Ideally, it will be introduced when the child is about two years old. You will make a simple statement such as "We are going inside to eat lunch in two minutes, so please finish your chalk drawing" and hold up two fingers. When you make this statement, you make eye contact with the child and check for understanding. You refrain from making this statement until you know for sure that you are, indeed, transitioning in two minutes. During this two-minute period, show your intent to leave by gathering up your belongings, etc. Once two minutes pass, you collect your child and leave. Initially, your child may be resistant to this structure. However, if you start this when your child is small and portable, you can simply scoop up your resisting child and leave the premises quietly, sending a firm message that you are, in fact, transitioning from one activity to another. Parents who have adopted the authoritative parenting style described in Chapter 5 find this to be a very effective strategy.

> Two-Minute Rule: Tell your child that a transition will be occurring in two minutes. "Son, we're leaving the playground in two minutes." And with this statement, you hold up two fingers and check for comprehension.

Over time, the two-minute rule can evolve into a simple statement and two raised fingers. In response, your child can hold up two fingers in return, demonstrating understanding and better listening.

In contrast, the *two-more-times* rule consists of setting a boundary for the child, after which a transition is going to occur. Now, I refer to it as the "two-more-times" rule, but you can insert the appropriate number for your situation. For example, "Swing ten more times on the swing and then we're going" or "Take five more licks of your ice cream cone and then throw it away" or "Go down the slide two more times and then we're leaving." Clear expectations about when the transition is going to occur are established, and your consistent follow-through guarantees that your child will comply. If you're at the park and you've just set a "slide two more times" rule, stand at the bottom of the slide, clap and cheer when they successfully slide, and gather them up quickly to get them to the car. There is no negotiating or power struggle, which will reduce the possibility of a temper outburst. If they do resist, set a natural/logical consequence and follow through: "If we don't leave now, we're not coming back to the park tomorrow afternoon," for example. As Chapter 6 states, avoid chasing whenever possible.

Bedtime

Ah, bedtime. One of the primary reasons parents contact me. Mess with Mom and Dad's sleep and fatigue, irritability, and a sense of hopelessness become powerful motivators to get parenting support.

Some parents struggle with bedtime because they've established a pattern of co-sleeping and they now wish to transition the child to their own bed. Other parents simply need support to teach and motivate their child to go to bed (and remain in bed!) without drama. As noted in Chapter 2, chronic sleep deprivation and an inability to self-soothe when wakened are significant predictors for behavioral problems among children of all ages. Therefore, it's important to establish a nighttime routine that results in your child obtaining high-quality sleep for an appropriate length of time.

The following section discusses the steps to creating a bedtime routine that 1) transitions your child from *your* bed to *their* bed (if that's a relevant issue for you) or 2) results in the child going to bed and *staying in bed* without getting up or engaging in a temper outburst:

Preparing for a New Bedtime Routine

1. Make their bedroom more appealing.

Let your child pick out his bed sheets. Supply a night light. Make sure there are no weird or scary noises emanating from somewhere, such as a ticking clock, rattling vent, or curtains getting rustled by a ceiling fan. Place a family photo next to the bed. Get your child a sound machine. Basically, eliminate any factors that could possibly turn into excuses as to why they can't simply remain in their bed and go to sleep.

2. Make your bedroom less appealing.

If your child is an unwelcome co-sleeper, start sending the message that your bedroom is "your" space. Keep the door shut during the day. Clear it of your child's belongings. Don't allow the children to play in your room or misuse your belongings (such as jumping or eating on your bed). Make sure you refer to it as "Mommy and Daddy's room." Remove any night lights. If you have a television, refrain from watching children's shows on it (or refrain from using it at all while the children are present). Suggest that they ask permission to enter your bedroom, either with a verbal request or by knocking. Basically, take all the fun out of your bedroom.

3. Introduce the idea.

Give them advance warning and rely on nurturing communication to explain and soothe. Talk about how now that they're _____ years old, they're a "big boy/girl" and they need to start sleeping in their own bed and/or going to bed without exiting their room or crying. Point out peers or siblings who sleep in their own bed without fuss. Discuss it openly with family members and teachers: "Mrs. Wilson, did you know that soon Natalie is going to be sleeping in her own bed every night?" Describe the benefits, such as how they'll get to have friends sleep over. If they express anxiety or fear, acknowledge their feelings—"I know you're worried about feeling lonely after we say goodnight"—but reframe the negatives into positives whenever possible: "You won't be so sleepy in the morning when you get up to go to daycare." Potential natural consequences can be discussed, such as "Mom's getting cranky because she has to get up over and over to put you back in bed."

4. Set a date.

Look at the calendar with your child and set a date in the future when the new routine will begin. Pick a date that's no more than two weeks away. If your child's issue is co-sleeping, designate one night a week that you'll call "sleepover night," which means she gets to sleep with you on that particular night. If your child's issue is going to bed uneventfully, choose a night she can stay up an extra 30 minutes. Make sure to choose a night that is not a school night, and explain why, as school nights are not acceptable nights to change the routine. Once these nights are chosen, do not get talked into changing them, particularly at bedtime when the child cries, "I want tonight to be sleepover night!"

5. Make a plan.

In the days leading up to the "big day," discuss the bedtime routine. Talk about how they're going to change into their pajamas, brush their teeth, and choose a story to read. You will come into their room, sit on their bed with them (don't lie down or get under the covers—they will cling to you like a leech) and read the story. After you read the story, you'll arrange the room so that it best suits their sensory needs (night light, sound machine, door open or closed), turn off the light, give them three silly kisses, and leave the room. You'll promise that once they are asleep you will check on them and blow them a kiss. I strongly encourage you to make a poster that illustrates a picture of each step (see the example below).

Bedtime Steps Poster

Prior to the "big day," practice this exact routine during the day (not at bedtime, because you don't want to associate the bedtime routine with them getting out of their bed and coming into your room, as the child hasn't yet started to sleep in his own bed yet).

Also, decide on what the consequences will be if they don't comply with the routine and 1) engage in a temper outburst for an extended period of time or 2) get out of their bed and exit their bedroom. We'll talk about this next.

Transitioning to the New Bedtime Routine

Now that you've "set the scene" for a successful transition to their bed, you need to implement the plan. On the "big day," you should:

1. Wear them out during the day with physical activity.

Get them good and tired, but do not keep them up later than usual. You're trying to establish a routine, so set the tone.

2. Adhere to the routine that you've practiced.

Refer to the poster you created. Set the stage for intrinsic motivation by expressing pleasure and pride in your child for trying something new and potentially scary. If you feel so inclined, discuss how you plan to celebrate your child's first successful night in her own bed (consider the use of an extrinsic motivator, such as a doughnut for break-fast or a phone call to Grandma to tell her), but be prepared to withdraw the reward if she doesn't remain in her bed all night.

Troubleshooting

It is very possible that even with all of your advance preparation, your child will resist a change to his or her bedtime routine. The following are some potential reactions and suggestions for handling them.

If you put your child to bed and she begins engaging in a temper outburst, you have three choices:

1. Ignore for as long as it takes (preferred).

2. Ignore for 15 minutes, enter the room and offer verbal comfort (don't pick her up or get into the bed with her), then leave again after three or five minutes. Realize that when it's time to leave, your child is unlikely to have calmed down and you'll end up leaving her crying.

3. Abort plan and recognize that your child will probably sleep with you until she's a preteen and is super motivated to go on sleepovers.

If you put your child to bed and he fails to stay in his bed *but he remains in his bedroom*, you have three options:

1. If your child exits his bed and remains in his room, ignore him. If he turns on the lights and/or begins playing with his toys, ignore him for the first night and then unplug all his lights the next day (except a night light) and remove some of his preferred toys. This is limiting his ability to engage in a power struggle, which has the added bonus of boring him into submission.

2. If your child exits his bed and lies on the floor, kicking and screaming, ignore. He's in his room (not your bed). Consider it a success. After several nights of falling asleep on the floor after a crying jag, he'll become motivated to creep back into his bed.

3. Abort plan and recognize that your child will probably sleep with you until he's a preteen and is super motivated to go on sleepovers.

If you put your child to bed and he *exits his bedroom,* you have two options:

1. With minimal use of words ("Get back to bed, Alex"), guide him back to his room, tuck him into bed matter-of-factly, and leave the room. Do not lose your temper or coddle him. It's bedtime, not social time, and you have nothing for which to apologize. This choice could result in your going back and forth to his room dozens of times, as he's likely to keep getting up and exiting his room because it's very fun to make Mom or Dad keep jumping up all evening.

2. Give him one warning, then shut his door. ("Alex, if you choose to come out of your room after bedtime, then your door will be shut.") Once the door is shut, it stays shut for the remainder of the night. He can "earn" the right to keep his door open the following night if he makes the choice to remain in his room.

If your child has his door shut and he still comes out, then you're officially in a power struggle (see Chapter 6), as now you've set an expectation (stay in your room) and he's actively defying you. You need to remove the potential to engage in a power struggle by one of three ways:

1. When you shut the door, hold it closed with your hand. He'll try the door, cry and scream, and eventually give up and go back to bed or fall asleep lying next to the door.

2. Place a safety knob on the door handle on the inside of the door (the kind one uses with toddlers to prevent them from opening doors) to prevent him from being able to open it. Depending on his age, this may not be a deterrent.

3. Replace the door knob with one that locks on the outside. If he exits his room, the door can be shut and locked. This approach clearly eliminates the power struggle, although many parents aren't comfortable with it. Please be reassured that the door will only need to be locked a handful of times before the child understands that 1) they can *choose* whether the door is shut and locked because it will *only* be locked if they exit their room *after* you've said goodnight and left the room, or 2) it's no fun to be locked in your room, and he doesn't want to have that repeated again. For this to work, it needs to be administered consistently. This intervention is very effective, but it's hard on Mom and Dad.

And yes, your child might rip apart his room in his anguish over having to sleep in there by himself. You may want to clear out any breakables or valuables prior to implementing this plan.

Taking Care of Personal Belongings/Cleaning Up

One of the earliest ways in which parents attempt to impart responsibility is by requiring children to clean up their toys. Starting with the "clean up" song chanted by teachers in preschool classrooms and ending with the parent who nudges their slumbering teenager as they occupy a bedroom littered with clothes, grooming products, and electronics, a primary aspect of raising children appears to be encouraging them to clean up one mess after another.

Rule #1: Teach your children how to take care of their belongings.

Like any other preferred behavior, taking care of belongings is a skill that needs to be taught. A parent can't simply direct their child to "clean up" and expect her to know how to do so in a productive, time-efficient way. Here are some strategies that may be helpful:

1. Get them started.

Tell them to start by cleaning up five things. It may be five DVDs. Or five hair bows. Or five puzzle pieces. Any five items will do. Once they do this, praise them and encourage them to clean up five more. If you feel their motivation start to flag, tell them, "You pick up five things, and I'll pick up five things. Let's work as a team." As they take these mini-steps and see the room get cleaner, they'll feel less overwhelmed and therefore be more likely to persist past the five things prompt.

2. Clearly communicate your expectations.

Tell them to start by cleaning up one type of item. "Pick up all the pants off the floor and fold them." "Pick up all the items that belong to the kitchen set." If they're very little, they may need hand-over-hand assistance (you take your toddler by the hand and in a loving, gentle, sing-song way, press their little hand to an item, scoop it up, and put it where it belongs. Once it's in place, you cheer to reinforce and immediately encourage them to pick up another toy).

3. Set a time limit.

If your children are older and the house has gotten to that disheveled, water-glasses-on-every-surface-and-whose-papers-are-these? state, it may be time for a "family cleanup." In this situation, you gather your family members, give everyone a specific task ("Claire, you go into every room, pick up every dish or glass, and bring it to the kitchen sink. Dylan, you drag everyone's dirty clothes hamper to the laundry room and start the first load of laundry. I'm going to empty the dishwasher and start loading it"), and then set the timer for a specific time frame (for younger children, age eight and younger, the time frame will be brief, such as 10 or 15 minutes). Once the timer goes off, the "cleaning time" is done. If the house is particularly messy, you can always add in another cleaning time later in the day or the next day. To foster the team spirit mentality, encourage each child to complete a task that benefits the entire family and helps take care of the house in a general sense.

4. Let logical consequences play a role.

If your children are consistently careless with their belongings, scoop their things up into a box and set the box out of sight (the garage is a favorite area). They can either go outside and retrieve them, or you can require them to *earn* them back. For example, to earn back the baseball jersey that was left lying on the bathroom floor, they can fold a load of laundry or tidy up the bathroom. Feel free to pick a chore that relieves you of one of your responsibilities—after all, you lost the time it took you to clean up the jersey, pack it into the box, and store the box in the garage. Note: This strategy is most effective when used with items that have been repeatedly misused. Otherwise it just seems mean.

Rule #2: Those who don't take care of their toys don't deserve toys.

One of the most upsetting aspects of your child's being careless with his belongings is *watching* it. Seeing the mess on the floor. Knowing that the pieces will be lost. Anticipating something getting broken. So stop watching it.

Taking care of toys and personal belongings is a sign of respect—respect for the toy, respect for the person who purchased it, and respect for the income that paid for it. Once children are older than four or five, most can understand that the consequence of losing and breaking toys is that there are fewer toys with which to play.

Keep in mind, however, that this is a difficult rule to enforce if Mom and Dad don't respect their own belongings. If Dad's closet floor is covered with wrinkled, dirty clothes and Mom's car has remnants of a dozen lunches on the go, it may be better to set a family goal, rather than pointing fingers at the irresponsibility of the youngest members.

However, the concept is simple: If you don't take care of it, it goes away. You can let natural consequences evolve and watch your child lose or break one item after another, or you can simply take the toy away if you see it being mistreated. In our home, anything that's treated carelessly may be picked up by Mom and put away for an extended period of time. This consequence is presented with compassion, as it's assumed that a child who is careless with his toys isn't quite developmentally ready to have so much responsibility. And once the toy is lost or broken, it isn't replaced.

Dealing with Whining

Oh, the whining. Every statement, no matter how neutral, sounds grating and unpleasant when uttered in a whiny tone. And children will almost always default to whining if it's permitted. From my perspective, whining is disrespectful, as it's often associated with a request that sounds querulous and demanding when stated in a whiny tone.

1. *Make a point to notice the whining.*

Whining, in children, can sneak up on you. It often begins prior to the formation of decipherable words. First the toddler points and says, "Eh-eh-eh." Mom and Dad, proud and relieved that their child can finally express herself, jump to accommodate. If Mom or Dad doesn't meet their child's needs immediately, the "eh-eh-eh" will progress into an insistent "EH-EH-EHHH" that quickly degenerates into full-out whining. By the time the child speaks formal language, the whiny pre-speech sounds are firmly established and transition effortlessly into whiny words, phrases, and sentences.

> If whining is going to be remediated, it needs to be noticed each time so it can be responded to immediately and in a consistent manner.

However, because whining seeps into the child's mode of communication surreptitiously, parents often don't "hear" it. Or they only hear it after it approaches nearly unbearable decibels or occurs for no apparent reason. Think of the parent who can tune out the child who says, "DaddyDaddyDaddyDaddyDaddyDaddy" in the car 4,345 times on the way home. Eventually he will turn around and bark, "What?" because it will finally break through his unconscious and become irritating.

Therefore, parents need to make a point to notice the whining as it's occurring. Only then can it be addressed effectively.

2. Supply a replacement behavior—teach them what to do instead of whining.

Each time your child whines, respond by saying, "No whining, please. Use your 'big boy (girl)' voice." Then repeat the child's original statement in a cheerful, respectful, non-whiny tone. If your child repeats her statement in a non-whiny tone, praise her ("Ahhh, that's better. There's my sweet girl's nice voice!") and try to accommodate her request. If she refuses to repeat her original statement in a non-whiny tone, simply say, "I can't hear you when you say it in a whiny tone. I'll help you when you can ask me in your big girl voice." The goal is to refrain from reinforcing the misbehavior while teaching a prosocial replacement behavior.

When your child is prompted to use her "big girl" voice every time, she will soon get tired of having to repeat everything and will default to speaking in a non-whiny tone. Eventually, the "big girl" voice will became the standard mode of communication.

Restaurant Etiquette

While busy parents often resort to drive-through and take-out food to feed hungry kids, a good source of family time consists of sharing a sit-down meal at a restaurant—preferably a restaurant not plagued by misbehaving children who eschew eating in favor of leaving their seat, whining, having temper outbursts, or using poor table manners.

As with every behavior we've discussed, we first need to make sure that children know *how* to behave in a restaurant. To teach this skill, it may be helpful to role-play a scene from a restaurant in which they practice taking a seat, ordering their food, brainstorming ideas as to how to entertain themselves while waiting for their food, and using appropriate manners. In addition, there are several factors described below that, if implemented, can ensure a positive dining experience. You'll notice that most of these factors are mirroring the concepts illustrated in Chapter 3 during the discussion of the Whole Child:

1. *Choose a family-friendly restaurant.*

To avoid an unwelcome debate about restaurant preferences, parents may wish to choose the restaurant or give a limited number of dining options. If the child complains, he can be offered the choice to remain at home with one parent (key point: and make their own dinner), while the rest of the family goes out and brings the at-home parent take-out from the chosen restaurant (which the parent will then enjoy without offering any to the complaining child, who now probably thinks the previously rejected food looks delicious).

Note that the restaurant chosen by the parents should be child-friendly in order to elicit better behavior. These restaurants typically have a kid's menu, fast service, and servers and patrons who don't cringe at the sound of a child who struggles to use an "inside voice." Expecting your three-year-old child to act outside of his developmental age so you can linger over a glass of wine and stimulating conversation with another adult is unrealistic and will just leave you frustrated and hungry.

2. *Set the stage for success.*

Consider your child's sensory needs. If your child missed her nap that day and is super fussy, hungry, or tired, don't expect to achieve behavioral success. At minimum, feed her a small snack to keep her from feeling miserably hungry while waiting for her food.

3. *Pay attention to your child.*

The act of being in a restaurant isn't inherently entertaining. Even if you have chosen a family-friendly restaurant with relatively speedy service, plan to engage your child in conversation or a quick game of peek-a-boo, tic-tac-toe, or I Spy. Don't expect him to sit in his seat without any stimulation while you chat with your adult companion.

4. *Be prepared.*

Similar to number 3, arrive at the restaurant prepared. Have some hand sanitizer so you're not forced to stumble around with your children in a public restroom. Bring some Uno cards or some coloring materials. Don't go at the busiest time on a Saturday night. Like any activity, dining out will go more smoothly if you have the right materials and factor in timing.

5. *Prior to entering the restaurant, give an advance warning about the behavioral expectations.*

Tell them that you expect them to remain in their seat and use a quiet voice so they don't bother the other diners. Tell them that you'd like to be engaged with them, but if the adults are talking, they need to be courteous and not interrupt. Remind them of the manners that you will be looking for (for example, they need to use their napkins, chew with their mouths closed, and use their utensils). Describe your behavioral expectations specifically and cheerfully with the assumption that they are planning to adhere to them. You aren't fostering a nurturing communication style if you sit in the parking lot and scold your children before they've even done anything wrong.

6. *Explain the potential consequences of misbehavior and be prepared to follow through with these consequences.*

Because attention is inherently reinforcing, misbehavior should not be addressed by supplying excessive attention (although if you see "signs" of potential misbehavior, you may need to ask yourself if you're paying enough attention to your child). If your child misbehaves, she should be given one warning and reminded of the potential consequences. If she continues to misbehave, the following responses will be helpful:

> Throughout this book, we discuss the need to "ignore." Ignoring is withdrawing attention in a neutral manner. Ignoring does not consist of not engaging with your child while you stomp around, sigh, and speak ill of your child to other people present.

a. One parent should remove the child from the restaurant immediately. The child should be taken to the car, buckled into her seat, and ignored. The child's food should be abandoned. The child should not be rewarded by having special one-on-one time with the parent by engaging her in conversation, listening to music, taking a walk, or otherwise doing something appealing. The other parent (if another adult is present) should remain in the restaurant (with the remainder of the behaving children, if applicable). This parent can box up the other parent's food (leaving the misbehaving child's food). Basically, you are putting the child in a time-out in the car.

b. If the child is having a temper outburst and is excessively loud, make sure she is safe and exit the car, demonstrating to her that you are not attending to her misbehavior (for example, you may wish to lean against the car with your back to your child and peruse your smartphone).

c. When the parent/children who were left in the restaurant exit, the time-out is over (if the child is not hysterical or out of control). The child will not be permitted to re-enter the restaurant or claim her abandoned food.

How to Say "Yes" as a Way to Motivate Your Child

"Can I have a snack?"
"Can you play a game with me?"
"Can you get that down for me?"
"Can you help me?"

All day, your child peppers you with requests. Sometimes, the answer is no, unequivocally. Many times, the answer is yes. You could simply say "yes" and move on with your day, but doing this doesn't capitalize on an opportunity to seamlessly incorporate a routine task into your current activity. Therefore, I like to encourage parents to say yes with a caveat. The caveat is to say yes, *but add on a request that fulfills a routine task that they're going to be asked to do in the near future.*

> *"Absolutely. I'll get you a snack while you put away your book bag and shoes."*
> *"Good idea. I'll find your soccer jersey; you get out your math homework."*
> *"Definitely. Run and tell your sister it's time for dinner, and I'll get you some milk."*
> *"Sure. Get your shower out of the way, and I'll set up the game while you're in there."*
> *"Yes, I'd be happy to. Can you peek in your bedroom and make sure there are no wet towels on the floor?"*

Clearly, the answer to each question is "yes", and the child recognizes this. But you've structured it so that a less preferred activity must be completed prior to granting his request. This is motivating as long as the request is reasonable (i.e., It doesn't take too long and is not excessively unappealing. For example, a child isn't going to feel motivated to complete two hours of homework after he's asked you to retrieve his baseball mitt from a high shelf in the garage).

Parents often use this strategy in an overt manner, such as "Sure, you can have dessert if you eat your green beans" or, "I'll help you with your math after you take out the garbage," but this more closely resembles bribery. In contrast, my suggestion is more subtle, as it requires the parent to be vigilant about using each request from their child as an opportunity to motivate him to do a less preferred activity that will inevitably occur.

> **"Yes with a caveat" is based on Premack's principle, which states that a highly desired activity can be used as a reinforcer for a less desired activity.**

This strategy prevents you from saying yes to something (such as playing a game) and then soon after trying to cajole your child into completing a routine task, such as putting on his pajamas or cleaning up a small mess. If your response is administered in a casual, cheerful tone, your child is more likely to comply quickly and without complaint versus noticing that you're making him do something boring before he gets to do something appealing. If your child does protest, it's easy enough to point out that you've said yes to his request—he just needs to also say yes to yours.

Fostering Respect

Oftentimes, while in public or with a client, I'll observe disrespect between a parent and a child. They may speak to each other in a harsh tone. They may not make eye contact. They may be demanding and bossy, rather than polite and inquiring. They may fail to use praise or compliments, refrain from saying "please" and "thank you," and use sarcasm in a hurtful manner. In homes such as these, only the parent can change this dynamic, as their role-modeling or disrespectful behavior has most likely contributed to the current situation.

Other times, I hear the parent speak in a gentle, kind tone, while their child is demanding and harsh. In these situations, it's apparent that the parent's accommodating nature is simply being exploited, as the child has learned that treating her parent poorly has no ramifications—she simply gets what she wants faster as her parent attempts to appease her over and over. As described in Chapter 5, this kind of permissive parenting is ineffective. The fact is, you'll be treated how you let yourself be treated. If your child speaks to you disrespectfully and you accommodate her (or at minimum, don't address it), then you are, in effect, giving her permission to speak to you that way. You're reinforcing the behavior.

But rather than accommodate your child when she's being bossy or demanding and then lose your temper and yell something like, "Don't talk to me like that!" (which is simply mimicking the disrespectful behavior that you're protesting), you need to send a consistent message. You will not respond or address any needs voiced by a child who speaks disrespectfully to other people. If you detect disrespect, you will first offer her a replacement behavior: "Please don't speak to me that way. Ask me nicely. I'd like you to say, 'Mom, can you help me tie my shoes, please?'" If she will not reframe her question or comment to reflect a respectful tone, then you can 1) ignore her or 2) place her in time-out.

Common Behavioral Strategies to Avoid

There are two behavioral strategies that I never recommend for parents. In my experience, they are ineffective and exhausting.

Token Economy

The first is called a "token economy." This is when you create a chart that lists responsibilities or desired behavior (for example, it may be a chore chart or a list of one or two behavioral expectations, such as "keep your hands and feet to yourself") and give a tangible reward when the child adheres to the requirements.

	Monday	Tuesday	Wednesday	Thursday	Friday	Saturday	Sunday
Uses Big Kid Voice	X	X		X	X	X	X
Uses Words, Not Hands and Feet		X	X		X	X	X
Puts Away Toys		X		X		X	
Clears Plate from the Dinner Table	X	X	X	X	X	X	X

They almost never work in the home environment for the following reasons:

1. They're hard to implement.

They're boring and tedious both for the child and the parent who is trying to monitor them. You are basically required to do something effortful when the child behaves. Typically when a child behaves, our natural inclination is to do nothing and just enjoy it. While I've discussed on numerous occasions that parents must attend to and reinforce their child when he is behaving appropriately, I think a token economy system makes praise seem so much less genuine when it's accompanied by a trip to the wall in the kitchen so that a sticker can be placed in a box. It interferes with the goal of encouraging a behavior to progress from being extrinsically motivated to intrinsically motivated.

2. Because they're hard to implement, they're rarely implemented consistently.

So many parents will say, "Another behavioral therapist told us to do a behavioral chart, and it worked well for four days, then it stopped working." Careful questioning reveals that after the first handful of days, the parents skipped opportunities to reward with a tangible item, or they couldn't because the behavioral chart was at home and they were at the store, or because the child misbehaved one time and then got completely discouraged because they now had a big empty box on their chart.

3. The "token" has to be chosen very, very carefully.

Token economies rely on a tangible reward. It may be something like, "If you earn five stickers, we'll go for ice cream" or, "If you earn three stickers, you'll get to have a friend over," etc. However, parents often do one of two things: 1) choose a reward that the child doesn't find motivating at all (not all kids like candy) or 2) choose a reward that is annoying or difficult for the parent to implement (for example, parents don't necessarily want to play a game for 30 minutes every single night of the week when they have a big deadline looming at work. Their frustration and impatience at playing Candy Land over and over will seep into their interaction with the child, and the child will detect it. This is basically turning reinforcement into punishment because no one is having fun).

Competition

The second behavioral strategy that I never recommend to parents is using competition, especially between siblings. In this scenario, a parent may say to a child, "Okay, let's see how fast you can get your shoes and coat on . . . ready, set, go!" The parent hopes that a little friendly competition will be motivating. I think it tends to backfire.

1. Family members should not be pitted against one another.

One child is not superior simply because he can put his shoes on faster, but he feels that way when he's praised for doing something quicker or better than his sibling. And if one sibling feels superior, the other sibling probably feels inferior. And siblings shouldn't make each other feel that way. Families are teams, not rivals. And loyalty and support should be encouraged and role-modeled.

2. It's hard to orchestrate the setting so each sibling can demonstrate a strength.

When you have siblings compete, the older sibling almost always wins. She is bigger, more advanced developmentally, and more experienced. Of course she can carry her milk to the counter without spilling it more successfully—her coordination is better. Of course she can get up the stairs to take a bath quicker—she can run faster and may actually plow over her brother along the way. There's no sense in fostering pride in your older sibling for having a skill that she only has because she's older or bigger. And parents will make themselves crazy trying to generate a scenario where their younger/weaker/less practiced child can triumph over his older sibling.

3. Some things shouldn't be rushed.

Even if you only encourage your children to compete over certain tasks, they tend to generalize it to everything. Homework, showering, and chores are several examples of things that benefit from being done in a mindful way. No one wants their child to write an essay in five minutes flat and then expect praise when he slams down his pencil and screeches, "I'm done!"

Conclusion

Parenthood is a role that's never ending and never truly mastered. Fortunately, it's a task that leaves much room for variation, as there is no single path to becoming a "good" parent. However, as this book recommends, there are general characteristics that can be adopted by parents to help ensure that each family member maximizes their potential to feel loved, supported, and respected. The principles I've described have helped hundreds of families function more effectively, and my primary goal as a clinician and author is to convey my suggestions in a manner that feels relevant, achievable, and insightful.

In my personal life as a parent, I strive to establish a flourishing family dynamic that's comprised of healthy boundaries between parent and child, an overall understanding of the Whole Child, consistent reinforcement of positive behavior, and the use of a nurturing communication style. "Respect" is a word that's uttered often in our home, as I frequently find it lacking in other areas of life, even where love is abundant. While my goal is for my children to feel loved, supported, and respected, I also strive to teach them that relationships take work—we need to be present and mindful in our dealings with one another. Our successes should be celebrated and our missteps should be forgiven. Our words have an impact and our actions have consequences. We can operate as individuals while remaining engaged in a larger family framework. I want them to understand that the parent-child relationship should be mutually satisfying, even if our roles are drastically different.

Lastly, I'd like to encourage you to look at your children and recognize their strengths. Celebrate that while their triumphs are most certainly theirs to savor, you've greatly contributed to their formation. Set aside your worries and fears as a dedicated parent and revel in everything you've done *exactly right* since the onset of parenthood. We always take time to lament our mistakes, but I encourage you to start the next chapter of parenthood with the inherent belief that you, while a work in progress, are exactly what your children need.

Key Points Discussed in Chapter 9

- Children need to be taught how to make transitions. Once they know how, they need to be motivated to do so. Two helpful strategies are 1) the two-minute rule and 2) the "two-more-times" rule.

- When it comes to bedtime, the theme of "Don't let your child do today what you don't want to them to do tomorrow" is extremely relevant. This chapter describes a step-by-step plan for how to transition your child from your bed to their own, as well as how to get your child to go to bed each night without a lot of drama.

- When it comes to taking care of personal belongings, remember that "Those who don't take care of their toys don't deserve toys." But in order for this to be reasonable, children need to be taught how to take care of their toys *and* parents need to role-model respect toward their own belongings.

- Whining can't be remediated unless it's addressed each time it occurs. Parents need to insist that their children use their "big kid" voice as a replacement for whining.

- Like all prosocial behavior, restaurant etiquette needs to be taught. This can be done most effectively through the use of role play. Once children understand the behavioral expectations, parents can encourage appropriate behavior by choosing an appropriate restaurant, considering their child's sensory needs, attending to them in the restaurant, giving advance warning of potential consequences, and following through with what has been stated.

- "Yes with a caveat" is a strategy based on Premack's principle, which states that a highly desired activity can be used as a reinforcer for a less desired activity. However, the caveat must be reasonable and not excessively unappealing.

- No request that is presented disrespectfully should be granted.

- There are two behavioral strategies that I avoid recommending to parents: the use of a token economy system and the use of competition as a motivator within families.

Notes: _____

References

Baumrind, D. (1967). Child care practices anteceding three patterns of preschool behavior. *Genetic Psychology Monographs, 75,* 43-88.

Chapman, G. D. (2010). *The 5 Love Languages: The Secret to Love That Lasts.* Chicago: Northfield Publishing.

Children and Sleep (n.d.). Retrieved 6 March 2012 from www.sleepfoundation.org.

Hall, W. A., Scher, A., Zaidman-Zait, A., Espezel, H., & Warnock, F. (2012). A community based study of sleep and behavioural problems in 12 to 36 month-old children. *Child Care Health Development, 38* (3), 379-89.

Jolivette, K., Barton-Arwood, S., & Scott, T. M. (2000). Functional behavioral assessment as a collaborative process among professionals. *Education & Treatment of Children, 23* (3), 298-313.

Matricciani, L., Olds, T., & Petkov, J. (2012). In search of lost sleep: Secular trends in the sleep time of school-aged children and adolescents. *Sleep Medicine Review, 16* (3), 203-11.

Skinner, B. F. (1953). *Science and Human Behavior.* New York: Free Press.

Skinner, B. F. (1969). Contingency management in the classroom. *Education, 90* (2), 93-100.

Sugai, G. & Horner, R. H. (1999). Discipline and behavioral support: Practices, pitfalls, and promises. *Effective School Practices, 17,* 10-22.

USDA's MyPlate. United States Department of Agriculture. Retrieved 6 March 2013 from www.choosemyplate.gov

More great books from the *What Now?* Series!

Lesson Ladder is dedicated to helping you prepare for life's most fundamental challenges. We provide practical tools and well-rounded advice that help you achieve your goals while climbing the personal or professional ladder—whether it is preparing to start a family of your own, getting your child potty trained, or learning a new kind of financial management.

I'm Having a Baby! Well-Rounded Perspectives
Collective wisdom for a more comforting and "balanced" understanding of what to expect during pregnancy, childbirth, and the days that follow. $16.99

I Had My Baby! A Pediatrician's Essential Guide to the First 6 Months
Gain confidence to experience the true joy of parenthood! From learning what to expect during those first minutes in the hospital through your baby's first 6 months, this concise, reader-friendly, and reassuring guide covers core topics you'll need to know as a new parent. $16.99

I'm Potty Training My Child: Proven Methods That Work
Respecting that children and parenting styles differ, we created this guide to offer a variety of effective training solutions to help today's busy parents with easy, fast reading, and even faster results! $12.99

Making Kid Time Count for Ages 0–3: The Attentive Parent Advantage
Whether you're a working or stay-at-home parent, this book shows you how to maximize your time with your baby or toddler, with tips for developing a strong parent-child relationship and ways to ensure strong cognitive, social, and emotional development for your child. $16.99

Call toll-free to order! **1-800-301-4647**
Or order online: **www.LessonLadder.com**

CPSIA information can be obtained at www.ICGtesting.com
Printed in the USA
BVOW11s1053101213

338647BV00003B/5/P